A heartfelt and wide-ranging series of encouragements for dealing with grief.

—*Kirkus Reviews*

•••

If there was ever a book that could be your true friend when you most needed one, this is that kind of book. Open these pages and you will find comfort and relief.

—Mira Ptacin, author of the award-winning memoir *Poor Your Soul*

•••

At a Loss is an important modern guide to navigating life after the passing of your baby during pregnancy or infancy. Dr. Rothert offers wisdom and real-life suggestions, drawing from her personal experience as well as the countless hours she has spent counseling other parents who have endured this unimaginable tragedy.

—Kiley Hanish, OTD, OTR/L; founder, Return to Zero: HOPE

This is a lovely and much-needed book. Donna Rothert takes an overwhelming experience and helps the reader process it a piece at a time. Her essays are little gems, thoughtful and practical, but also written with depth and humor.

—Jeanne Menary, EdD, founder and leader of Beyond Choice Support Group

...

I highly recommend this book to men, and really to any family member or friend who also experienced the loss of an unborn or new baby in their life. As dads, we too need a guide to help us unlock our feelings. Take Donna's hand and allow her to walk with you through the darkest night.

—Bruce Linton, PhD, founder of the Fathers' Forum and author of *Fatherhood: The Journey from Man to Dad*

...

Fortunately for us, Donna Rothert is not at a loss for words. In *At a Loss*, she speaks not only from clinical experience but also from personal experience, including a variety of voices to help us navigate the complexity of perinatal loss. Hers is definitely a comforting voice. As Rothert herself puts it, "Whoever and wherever you are, I'm sorry for your loss. I wish you comfort and I wish you strength."

—Monica Wesolowska, author of *Holding Silvan: A Brief Life*

At a Loss offers gentle guidance for anybody navigating the terribly tumultuous terrain of perinatal-related grief. Seemingly insurmountable sorrow is given a most sincere, respectful, and honoring reprieve throughout these pages. Readers will find solace in the soul-sourced wisdom as well a dedicated place to rest, connect, and recalibrate.

—Meghan Lewis, PhD, founding executive director, LGBTQ Perinatal Wellness Center

...

To chronicle your own painful and revealing search for meaning after pregnancy loss and to make your story intimate with the solitary hearts of other bereaved parents requires courage, clarity, and faith. Donna Rothert possesses these qualities. *At a Loss* also speaks to professionals. Her insights and observations will be valuable to those looking to help and support bereaved parents. Donna's book is a treasure. I highly recommend it to bereaved parents and the professionals providing their care.

—Molly A. Minnick, LMSW, co-author of
A Time to Decide, a Time to Heal

AT A LOSS

Finding Your Way After Miscarriage,
Stillbirth, or Infant Death

DONNA ROTHERT, PHD

OPEN AIR
BOOKS

OAKLAND, CALIFORNIA

Designed by Sara Christian

Printed in the United States of America

First Printing, 2019

ISBN 978-1-7334386-0-5

Open Air Books
Oakland, California

For Greta

CONTENTS

INTRODUCTION

Grief is a house
where the chairs
have forgotten how
to hold us
the mirrors how to
reflect us
the walls how to
contain us...

—Jandy Nelson, *The Sky Is Everywhere*

"Everything feels different."

"How do people get through this?"

"I can't imagine life without our baby."

Losing a baby, either during pregnancy or after, is the passing of a dream and the end of a particular journey. It can feel like life has gone off the rails and now our pain and fear color everything. It's an upsetting yet fitting reaction to the disappearance of something or someone so meaningful and so deserving of our heart. Part of us has shattered, and we may fear that we will never be whole again.

Pregnancies, however they come to be, are wrapped up in intimacy, vulnerability, and emotion. They speak to a possible relationship with someone who wasn't there before. A pregnancy starts us on a path, and it can have a surprising and compelling momentum. Pregnancies change us physically, emotionally, and hormonally. They change our identity and role in our family. And we never know for sure where all those changes will take us.

Because a pregnancy is a direction for our future as well as a physical status, it sparks strong emotions. It's normal and expected to get attached, and this can happen very quickly as we learn due dates, sex, genetic details, and physical developments. Even if we feel fear, physical discomfort, or ambivalence, those feelings usually coexist with a sense of connection to the pregnancy and the new course that has been charted.

Expecting a baby is a powerful and multifaceted experience. So when something goes wrong, the effects on us are complicated and profound. Such a loss is private and physical, and at the same time public and relational. Because the loss can have many different associations for any of us individually or as a couple, it's tricky for us to process. It can be challenging for others to know how to help us, and it can be hard for us to know how to help ourselves.

I know this because I've been through it myself. My first perinatal loss was more than seventeen years ago. I was at twenty-two weeks gestation, and the loss was discovered during a routine exam. That evening I was sent to the hospital to have labor induced. After I delivered my daughter the next day, I had time to hold her and look at her. The cause of death was later found to be a blood clot in the umbilical cord—something that doesn't happen often but does happen.

My second loss was six months later, at eight weeks gestation—a miscarriage that required some extra time and a number of medical appointments to work through physically. The two experiences were both similar and different. They were devastating and surreal—and ultimately, to my surprise, bearable.

Those losses have taken me to some challenging and unanticipated places as a woman, mom, and psychotherapist. My experience has carved out spaces within me that resonate when I hear the stories of those who have lost someone so small—and yet something so big—that it brought them to their knees.

When I became a bereaved mother, I was also a psychologist, and my personal experience led me to specialize in working with those affected by pregnancy and infant loss. In the years since, working with women and couples who have known these types of losses, I've been honored to hear the stories of so many people from a variety of backgrounds. These women and men continue to add to my understanding of both the differences between those of us who have lost a pregnancy or baby and, I think more importantly, the striking, recurrent similarities among us on our shared journeys. It has also made me passionate about giving voice to these experiences that are all too often invisible or minimized.

This book is an extension of my life experience and my clinical work with perinatal loss. It includes thoughts from both the couch and therapist's chair about what it's like to live the hours, days, weeks, months, and years after losing a baby.

At a Loss is for you if you feel as if your life is forever divided between the time when you were expecting and the time when you had to start living in a very unexpected new reality. It's for you if you are feeling overwhelmed after your loss and unsure if what you're feeling is normal. It's for you if you are wondering if you'll ever feel better. It's for you if you need to know that you're not alone.

Let me say a word about language. "Perinatal loss" is a label for a category of pain that includes miscarriage, stillbirth, termination of a pregnancy due to prenatal diagnosis of a medical condition (affecting either the baby or the pregnant person), newborn death, and other reproductive loss. At times I will use the term "baby loss" to mean the same thing. Who we are and how we define our losses varies considerably, but we can benefit from knowing that many of us share feelings and challenges.

Going through a miscarriage is not the same as losing a baby through stillbirth, and they both have similarities to and differences from a pregnancy that is terminated for genetic reasons. It's hard to find words that fit all of these versions of heartbreak. I use "perinatal loss" and "baby loss" to indicate that we were attached to a pregnancy or baby and now are having to live without that pregnancy or baby. My intention is to help put words to the shared experiences of people affected by all of these kinds of reproductive losses.

Although those of us who have had a perinatal loss have many similar experiences, no one has the same life or the same loss. I'm a white, heterosexual woman who had her particular experiences of both an earlier miscarriage and a later (after twenty weeks) pregnancy loss. I had access to a support system of friends, family, and high-quality health care (although I still wish some of it had been medically better and more sensitive). My experiences, like yours, will have similarities and differences with all others who have lost pregnancies and babies.

You may be single or partnered, straight or LGBTQI+. You may have become pregnant through natural means or with assisted reproductive techniques that may have included others, such as donors or gestational carriers. You may be on the older or younger side of the reproductive years, and you could be from any racial, ethnic, and cultural background, any socioeconomic status or religious affiliation. This may be your first or tenth perinatal loss. You may have received compassionate, high-quality medical care—or not. You may be quietly grieving on your own, or you may be receiving tremendous support from family and friends. Whatever your circumstance, you are bringing your unique self and experience to it.

Of course, the pregnancy or baby you lost is unique as well. Your loss may have been early or late in pregnancy, or after delivery. You may have been expecting one baby, twins, or more. The pain you lived through may have been a sudden shock or a drawn-out crisis. You may have been given a medical explanation of what happened, or that piece may remain unknown.

Whoever you are in this journey of loss, you are unlike anyone else, but you are not alone.

Around the world, at this very minute, other people are grieving their baby losses and considering their futures. Although you may not feel very connected to them, you are likely churning through some of the same thoughts and feelings they are. It can be helpful to keep in mind that others are on this journey too, even if you don't have much contact with them. Taking a moment to acknowledge others living with similar losses, even from afar, can help you respect your own grief, which is a great start in your healing.

At a Loss consists of thirty short chapters, each exploring a different aspect of the road after perinatal loss. We'll look at how perinatal loss differs from other types of grief (for instance, there are physical consequences alongside the emotional ones, the loss may be hidden from others, and it tends to be minimized by society). We'll consider the emotional experience, from loneliness to anger and more. We'll look at taking steps back into the world (talking about it, returning to work, trying again) and how the loss affects your relationships (with your partner, family, friends, and coworkers). My hope is to help you begin to clarify parts of your own story to date and see some of the paths that may lie ahead. When you understand your past and present, it can be easier to accept yourself and the things that have happened to you, as well as to prepare for your future.

This book, like grief itself, is not linear. Each chapter stands on its own, but each is also interconnected. You can read as much or as little as you want, in whatever order you want. The quotes and vignettes may sometimes feel familiar to your current version of the world, or you may notice that you are seeing something in a new way. The chapters start with thoughts and words common among people who've experienced baby loss. You may find that some of them reflect your own experience, and you may notice that you view things differently. Either way is okay.

My hope is that this book will be a companion for you and support you in being a better companion to yourself, whether you're in the midst of a crisis or farther down the road of life after baby loss. Whoever and wherever you are, I'm sorry for your loss. I wish you comfort and I wish you strength. I also want you to know that by allowing yourself to consider and tolerate your feelings (even if it's just a bit at a time), notice your needs, and respect ways that you may have changed, you can find a place to hold your baby loss in the larger story of your life.

Chapter 1

EXPECTATIONS

Sometimes I think,
I need a spare heart to
feel all the things I feel.

—Sanober Khan

*"Why am I so upset
about losing someone
I didn't even know?"*

*"My partner isn't crying—
I don't think he's grieving in
a healthy way."*

"I will always feel like I do now."

When our lives have been sent off course by baby loss, our expectations of ourselves (and sometimes our partners) can be off as well. It's so easy to do a "pile on," giving ourselves a hard time for having a hard time. We may worry about grieving too slowly and wonder, *Am I dwelling on this?* or *How do I stop feeling this way?* We may worry about grieving too quickly and worry about "moving on" or "forgetting" or "betraying" the baby.

I remember having both feelings—being lost in the sorrow but at the same time feeling pressure to find my way out quickly and in a manner that worked for those around me. Unfortunately, there is nothing clear, clean, or elegant about the experience of early grief, with all of its pain, fear, and confusion. It often makes a mess of us, at least for a while, and we want it to stop. I wish I didn't know what I look like when I cry and brush my teeth at the same time, but, alas, from my time after losing my daughter, I do. It's just not a graceful phase of life.

Even if we've experienced significant loss before in our lives, we are all beginners in any fresh episode of grief. It's never fair to ourselves to expect that we are going to launch into some enlightened, graceful version of mourning after baby loss. Not right now, maybe not ever, and that's okay.

You don't have to be composed; you don't have to be skillful; you don't have to make anyone else comfortable. And there is no deadline when you have to be healed or back to "normal." Pressuring yourself or pretending will not get you to a better place faster and, sadly, that tactic may make things harder for you.

Moreover, you don't have to chase the very fraught goal of being "past" your loss or "finding closure," which may feel all wrong or like an insult to your experience and your understanding of baby loss.

So, what is a good starting point? What *should* you expect of yourself? I won't join the chorus of people telling you *how* to feel. Instead, what if you just notice *what* you feel? Whatever your emotional state is right now, it will change. The intensity of pain you experience in grief doesn't stay the same, because it can't.

Eventually, some other feeling will appear. The emotional song you are compelled to sing at any given moment may be one that makes you cry, yell, or withdraw a bit from the world, or it may be one that makes you smile, and the next song may be quite different. It's enough to keep a heart very busy. Whatever is pouring out of your heart, whatever your version of grief may be, it deserves your respect. Rather than running to an action or thought that might take you out of your grief, you—in fact, all of us— sometimes need to take a bow in reverence for your loss, your life, and your changed self.

Living with grief can certainly feel messy and chaotic. That *is* a reasonable expectation right now. It may make you feel a bit crazy to have your emotions become so unruly. But it's still you living a chapter of your life. You may be flooded with sadness about your past and reliving memories sweet or tragic. You may be full of hopes or heart-fluttering fears about your future. These are all signs of life. The next chapter of your life is going to be more of you living—and by surviving whatever you feel right now in this moment, you've already begun.

Chapter 2

THE BODY

Scars are just
another kind
of memory.

—M. L. Stedman, *The Light
Between Oceans*

*"The last thing I want
to look like right now
is pregnant."*

*"On top of everything else,
my milk came in."*

*"I feel hormonal and
my hair is falling out.
This seems like a cruel joke."*

Baby loss is unique in that there is, at least for a woman who has been pregnant, a physical experience that goes along with the emotional challenges. Nonpregnant partners and those working with the support of gestational carriers may also have strong reactions to the physical changes that occur during and after pregnancy as they witness them and empathize.

In all of my pregnancies, I felt a buzzing and humming in my body—different than it felt at any other time. It was a subtle but constant reminder that my physical and emotional selves were changed and changing further. Our hormonal weather and the shape-shifting of our bodies can be additional tangible reminders that we are expecting. If a pregnancy progresses to the point that we feel the movement of the fetus or baby, it can seem that a channel of communication has opened up as we receive the signals of action and growth.

These physical changes typically lead us to become more attached. When we're pregnant, there can be endless daily reminders of this changed status as we make more trips to the bathroom and adjust to a swollen belly or a different kind of walk. It's a cycle that reinforces our baby dream: we expect a baby; we physically change both internally and externally; we signal our changes to the people around us; and others, in turn, react to us as a mother- or parent-to-be.

However your pregnancy has ended, it was a physical experience. Hormonal changes after a pregnancy can send anyone with a healthy, living baby into postpartum depression or anxiety, and it can certainly contribute to the emotional challenges of losing a pregnancy or baby. Physical trauma and medical intervention—either experienced or witnessed—can vary considerably. So too can the psychological reactions to them. Taking some time to understand what you have been through physically and what it means to you is part of how you understand your story. It can also help you determine any ongoing needs—for example, physical therapy or a medical follow-up.

If your pregnancy lasted longer than the first trimester, lactation may be a part of the picture. As many women can attest to, having milk come in with no baby to feed can be crazy making. Along with being physically uncomfortable, the arrival of breast milk can be a harsh reminder of the version of life you expected, the one in which you were caring for your living baby.

The physical aspects of perinatal loss are echoing reminders of what we have been through. The embodied experiences may provide validation that something has changed and we are linked to what or who is missing. They can be unmistakable souvenirs of a life-changing trip to a different land. Our physical changes may also remind us of our openness and vulnerability. They can be the beginning of looking at who we are in a new post-pregnancy-with-no-baby life.

Our bodies are the pages on which our life story is written. Some of the physical scars, alterations, and reminders of perinatal loss will pass, and others (a C-section scar, stretch marks, a new or recently discovered risk for future pregnancies) will not. This truth parallels other parts of our loss story, as we pass through some parts of our grief, hold on to others, and come to terms with both our vulnerability and our strength.

Chapter 3

AMBIGUITY

I wanted a perfect ending. Now I've learned, the hard way, that some poems don't rhyme, and some stories don't have a clear beginning, middle, and end.

—Gilda Radner

*"Did my doctor put me on leave from work
because I had the procedure or
because I feel like my life is over?"*

*"I've heard the medical explanation,
but I still don't understand
how this could have happened."*

*"Did I have a miscarriage?
I don't even know what words to use."*

When you lose someone who was not known to
the world at large, the loss can be ambiguous and
confusing. This might be especially profound if you
had a miscarriage, stillbirth, or other loss during
pregnancy. It may be unclear to others in your life
whether the loss was a death or even an event of
great significance. It's especially complicated when a
pregnancy is ended due to dire medical news about
the baby or pregnant person. You may feel like you
don't have the right to say that you "lost" something or
someone because there was a termination procedure,
even though you desperately wanted your baby and
are grieving.

The ambiguity of losing a baby before it is born
is reflected in our lack of rituals for this kind of grief.

You and your loved ones may not know if you want a funeral or other ceremony. People may become tongue-tied around you or decide not to mention your loss at all. Work leaves may be based on medical need rather than bereavement, which can add to the confusion about what exactly we are going through and what we are supposed to do to recover. It can even be hard for others to find a sympathy card that's appropriate to send us.

A baby loss may not be recorded in a formal way. Depending on whether the loss was during or after pregnancy, whether a birth or death certificate was made, and who all was told, it may be an off-the-books experience. The fact that it may go undeclared and unwritten matches the potentially ambiguous quality of baby loss.

Not everyone who loses a pregnancy feels they have lost a baby. Not everyone who loses a pregnancy finds it to even be a big deal. But for most of us, it is an enormously big deal. It can feel like the invisible giant of losses, an earthquake that happened only to us. And understanding what it means to us—what was lost— may be a challenge to ourselves and to others.

Some aspects of the situation may be clear:

"My baby died."

"I'm not pregnant anymore. I won't be having a baby soon."

"I lost my dream of having this baby."

However, the specifics and scope of the loss may be quite confusing:

"Will I ever have a baby?"

"I lost a person! Is it okay to name my baby and to say I had a daughter?"

"Sometimes I feel like it was just part of me that I lost."

The confusing and amorphous nature of perinatal loss is expressed in the title of a book on pregnancy loss, *About What Was Lost*, edited by Jessica Berger Gross, and in the titles of two memoirs about carrying and losing a stillborn baby, *An Exact Replica of a Figment of My Imagination*, by Elizabeth McCracken, and *Ghost Belly*, by Elizabeth Heineman. The titles alone speak to an experience of losing someone who is both so precious and so ephemeral. These qualities make our losses a bewildering experience.

Pregnancy can feel like a complicated mix of physical and psychological changes. Whether you're an expecting woman or a partner, it's normal to feel shifts in your identity (for example, starting to see yourself as a mother) and a deepening attachment to your baby. The timelines for these experiences in pregnancy vary between each of us. If a particular pregnancy ends with a loss, the truck carrying all of your wishes, attachments, and expectations can't just back up to some earlier, pre-pregnancy place. You will be left carrying feelings from the pregnancy, whatever they may be. That's why an early miscarriage may feel like an unrealized dream or like the loss of a specific, loved baby.

Not every perinatal loss is seen as the loss of a person, and it doesn't need to be. We each have our own understanding of our loss, and we may feel it as a death or we may hold it more as the acute and painful disappearance of a dream or a version of our future. Legal definitions of personhood, medical procedures based on gestational age, and beliefs about when life begins don't start or stop attachments of the heart.

No one else has the right or ability to determine what your loss means to you. You don't have to adopt the words or explanations of others when deciding if you feel like you experienced the death of a person or death of a dream. Your pregnancy or baby was part of you, and you have the right to acknowledge (or discover) for yourself what the loss means to you.

Chapter 4

FEELING UNSEEN

I don't need a cloak
to become invisible.

—J. K. Rowling, *Harry Potter and
the Sorcerer's Stone*

*"We had a family gathering, and
no one mentioned the baby."*

*"It's been weeks since anyone checked in with
me to see how I'm doing."*

*"I told my friend I was having a hard day,
and she said she couldn't understand
why I was still so upset."*

When I was in my early twenties, one of my best
friends lost her second child. She was at full term with
a baby boy and found out just before delivery that
he had passed away. I had recently moved from the
Midwest to California and learned all of this from a
distance. As the details came in, I was sad, horrified,
and uncomfortably helpless. I was also, unfortunately,
too naive to really understand or empathize.

As a young, single woman who had no experience
with pregnancy or parenting, I could only try to imagine
what my friend was going through. It seemed surreal, like
something that would happen to people I didn't know. My
heart ached for her, and I repeatedly made brief, awkward
attempts to express my sympathy over the phone.

As I heard that my friend had named her son, visited
his grave daily, and spent much of her day crying,

I felt sympathetic—and then, within weeks, a bit uncomfortable and even judgmental. When the weeks turned into months, I continued to reach out with periodic, strained attempts at conversation, while my internal judgments grew louder. It seemed strange to me that she would grieve so intensely for someone who (I believed) had never truly been in the world. She didn't really know him, right? She already had one living child and certainly could expect to have more. Could she be making too much of her loss? Was she somehow making it worse? Might she be committing the crime (as we Midwesterners tend to see it) of being raw and open about intense feelings?

Kenneth Doka coined the phrase "disenfranchised grief" to refer to the pain of certain types of losses that are commonly unrecognized or minimized by society.[1] These include losses that society views negatively, such as the loss of a loved one through suicide, and those that are somehow hidden, such as a miscarriage.

Another type of perinatal loss is termination due to a prenatal diagnosis, such as a chromosomal abnormality that is incompatible with life or seriously threatens the quality of life. These losses are often experienced as a disenfranchised grief. Abortion— even when it may not feel like a choice—is a loss that many in our circle may view negatively. It may lead those of us in this situation to not even tell friends or family about our pregnancy or how and why it ended.

Support from family, friends, and even strangers is one of the ways we humans get through grief. When you have to grieve without these expressions of care and concern, you may feel the added burden of isolation on top of the the pain of missing your baby. If other people don't validate your strong feelings, you may feel ashamed of them. You are, in a sense, grieving without permission and without the recognition that your loss warrants a full experience of mourning.

Sometimes the expression of care isn't missing; it's inauthentic or inept. This, too, can add to your pain and suffering. To my knowledge, no one has ever felt helped by hearing (or sensing from their friend's unspoken communication) that she is overreacting to the loss of her baby. Grief is not a disease, it's not a choice, and it's certainly not something we can be talked out of.

In those moments when people just aren't there for you, or when they minimize your pain, it can help to know that it may be because they just don't understand your grief experience. It can also help to know that awareness of baby loss is growing and that, whether or not you have met them yet, there are people on your planet who understand why you are feeling the way you are feeling.

Your loss is understandably devastating, and it may be taking up much of your energy. You are having your own experience of grief, and you don't have to spend extra energy worrying that you are doing it right in the eyes of others. As Joanne Cacciatore writes in *Bearing the Unbearable,* "... if grief is a disease, so too must be love."[2]

Chapter 5

IDENTITY

In the social jungle
of human existence,
there is no feeling of
being alive without
a sense of identity.

—Erik H. Erikson

"Am I a mom?"

"I'm not the same person I used to be."

*"Being a dad made me a better person.
Since my baby died,
I feel like I've lost that too."*

After losing a baby, many of us notice that others seem to see us differently. And many of us say that we see *ourselves* differently, and we don't like what we see. Sometimes, after such a significant event, we're not quite sure who we are.

Seeing who we are at the present moment helps us get oriented to our values, our desires, and our place in the world. It also gives us a starting place to connect with others and be known to them.

Life events have the potential to shift how we view ourselves. Many of the men and women I see after a perinatal loss talk about feeling profoundly changed as a person as a result of the loss. These changes may feel dramatic and be difficult to describe. There are the permanent aspects of a changed life story ("I had a baby who died"), more fleeting experiences ("I am physically recovering from a miscarriage"), and pieces that may be much harder to categorize.

For example, if you are a woman who has gone through the nine-month physical and psychological process of pregnancy, you are not the exact same person you were before you became pregnant. If things had gone well up to the point of the loss, you were attaching to your child and preparing to parent that child, and your identity changed accordingly. Yet, if your baby died at birth, you may wonder if a childless mother is still a mother or if you have become something else. Additionally, when you've experienced a traumatic loss at a hospital, the medical setting and focus may have left you feeling more like a patient than anything else—as though the physical challenges were the main issue instead of the crisis of losing someone dear.

Not everybody who has experienced a perinatal loss feels that he or she is a parent to the lost baby. But for many, this identity as a kind of parent is a clear and important part of who they are. Many people have noted that there is no word to describe a person who has lost a child or children, whether during pregnancy or later in life—nothing along the lines of "orphan" or "widow" or "widower" to indicate that someone is missing and that the surviving person is living with an absence. Maybe this has something to do with the fact that it was more common in previous generations to lose young children. Whatever the reason, it can contribute to bereaved parents feeling like outsiders in a world that does not recognize them or their baby.

Many people have spoken to me about the trouble they have answering the question "Do you have children?" or "How many children do you have?" after a loss. The question can highlight a conflict or incongruence between how we see ourselves—whether as a parent, a bereaved parent, a grieving person, or a new, not-yet-named category of being in the world—and how we expect to be perceived by others. It may not always feel appropriate to launch into the longer explanation of our reproductive history and losses in the grocery checkout line or on the street, but I think it's important to ask and try to answer for ourselves who we are now.

So, who do you see in the mirror today? It's a complicated question under any circumstance. For those of us who have had our hearts demolished by baby loss, the lens through which we view ourselves and the world may be a little (or a lot) different than it was.

You may be clear about who you are in the aftermath of your loss, or you may still be putting the pieces together. You may see yourself as a person in a crisis or transition, as a grieving man or woman, a mom or dad missing a baby, or in some other way. Whether you want to announce it on social media, share it with close family and friends, or just acknowledge it to yourself, you might benefit from asking yourself and listening for the authentic answer.

Seeing who you are right now is another way of respecting yourself and your process. It also often opens your eyes to others who are in the same place. Making eye contact with that person in the mirror can help you to know your needs, communicate about yourself, and find your way in the world.

Chapter 6

PAIN & PERSPECTIVE

We must understand
that sadness is an
ocean, and sometimes
we drown,
while other days
we are forced to swim.

—R. M. Drake

"I've grieved before,
but I've never felt anything like this."

"Losing him has colored everything."

"Is this just going to be how I feel forever?"

When I see people in the midst of deep pain, the kind that is all-consuming, and hear about their attempts to negotiate interactions with the non-bereaved, I sometimes think about a scene from the movie *Return to Zero*. The film is based on a true story about a couple coping with the loss of their stillborn son.

This particular scene takes place some months after the loss, and the grieving woman, played by Minnie Driver, is in the midst of an alcohol-infused Thanksgiving dinner. At the table, family members start expressing gratitude for various things in their lives and making toasts. Following her father-in-law's elaborate and effusive toast "To life!" (during which Driver's character visibly sinks further into her own drunken sadness), she makes her own toast:

"I'm thankful that today I can see life for what it really is. To know that just beneath the surface, just under the radar, is death." She says a few more lines and ultimately raises her glass "to death!"

The words are sad, defiant, jarring, and clearly disturbing to some members of the family, but they make perfect sense to the bereaved couple. The toast seems to me to be a kind of postcard from the upside-down, acute-grief version of life, a version that needs to be acknowledged. Disinhibited somewhat by too many glasses of wine (which, by the way, I don't recommend as a coping mechanism), the grieving woman is giving voice to what is lost in her life.

Her speech acknowledges the baby who is dead, the part of herself that feels dead, and her acute awareness of the thin line between her losses and the right-side-up world of the others sitting around the table. The couple is living in the season of grief, which overrides any other dates on the calendar. And as sad as it is, their experience is just as real (and alive) as any other version of living. If those of us who grieve, or those around us, distance ourselves from that reality, it adds to our isolation and pain.

Most of us spend the majority of our lives traveling somewhere between the sentiments of the two toasts—the over-the-top shout-out to life and the dark nod to death. But we are likely to spend some significant time parked closer to one or the other of these perspectives. Someone is always parked near you, someone is always parked across the road, and we will all likely be switching positions at some point.

If you are in a season of grief, you may notice that you are looking at the world in a very different way than you have in the past. It also is likely to be very different than what you will experience in the future. This can be true even when you are convinced that all of your future days, months, and years will be as painful as this one.

There are people all over the world who are also grieving right now—people who feel just as sad and wrecked as you do, people who have also been made upside-down by a loss. Considering them with respect may help you to respect your own grief and have some compassion for yourself. You could connect with other travelers in the upside-down world just by shifting your awareness to consider them or, in a more hands-on way, by reading a memoir about baby loss or talking to someone who is in this same lousy club.

Baby loss covers both life and death, along with the drama and meaning in both ends of the human experience. We all want to live on the bright side, but since that's not a permanent address nor a complete description of a life, it may help us to keep our eyes and hearts open to toasts from both sides of the table.

Chapter 7
PLANS

Everyone has a plan
until they get
punched
in the face.

—Mike Tyson

"How soon should we try again?"

"We want to make sure we're grieving
as best we can
so we don't waste any time."

"I just need to know what to do next."

I am as fond of plan-making as the next person, and
I have a lot of admiration for my clients who are
planners extraordinaire. Many of those women
and men have developed and executed plan after
plan in their lives. They are often impressive plans.
Some people have prioritized and completed higher
education, some have found fulfillment in volunteer
work, some have traveled extensively, some have
developed exciting and rewarding careers, and some
have done all of the above.

The plans we make show something about us.
They are the hopes and intentions that we have
articulated and then been lucky and motivated enough
to manifest. The plans we make about our babies are
particularly special. These plans tend to involve our
most tender feelings of love and hope, and a desire
to care for someone. They are far reaching, shiny,
and beautiful. They involve dreaming on a big scale

for something dear—a conjuring of a new person, a beloved family member. And when the plans go awry, when we lose our babies, our world gets dimmer in a particularly painful way.

After baby loss, we're not in the best place to think about plans. We are hurt and knocked off course. Some energy is shifted away from thinking and doing and put into feeling. We stagger back and reevaluate what is and is not within our control. Stunned and wounded, we wonder what's next.

When confronted with the grief of losing a baby, we often want to jump right back into planning mode. We look for the fast track through grief, the shortcut, the best way of doing it. After all, we know how to get things done. If only we could think or plan our way out of pain. If only we could get some assurance of how long, how challenging this road will be and then get to the finish line as soon as possible.

I think we all have times when a brief moratorium on planning is in order. At least a temporary ban on heavy-lifting types of planning. It can be really hard to honor this ban. Anxiety and the desire to move on to some other experience may drive us to keep planning. The pain may feel unbearable.

You may have realistic concerns about wanting to try for another pregnancy soon due to age or other factors. You may be terrified of overwhelming sadness or other feelings that might occupy your time if you weren't busy making plans. These are understandable worries. And some distraction and denial is fine and even valuable. But grief is an experience whereby the maxim "You can run, but you can't hide" rings true. It's necessary to wander in the pain a bit without looking for the exit.

So what do I suggest you do instead of making more plans? I would start with spending some time breathing into your pain and uncertainty. Literally taking a breath with awareness is pretty much always a good idea during a stressful time. Doing so while acknowledging your pain and your resilience can be even more useful. I would encourage a respectful acknowledgment of the version of yourself who invested, who tried, who gave her heart to something so lovely. The innocent you who didn't know you were going to end up here deserves a moment of respect and notice.

Spend as much time as you want remembering your pregnancy or your baby in whatever way is right for you. For many people, finding ways to honor their baby is a lifelong priority, and this is a good time to start. It's also a way to honor yourself and your ability to love.

At some point you'll start working on some new plans. That's what we do. We move toward the future by zigzagging in the way we think will help us get to the place we think we want to be headed.

You may be especially fearful that your next plan will not work out. You may be especially aware of how wonderful it might be if it does. You may know that you have been changed by letting yourself have plans that were big enough to fail and still matter. You may take all of that in as you consider with compassion the sweetness of the dreams and plans you have had—and the ones yet to come.

Chapter 8

HOPELESSNESS

Luck always seems
like it belongs to
someone else.

—David Levien, *City of the Sun*

*"Of course, everyone else's pregnancy
will be fine—it's just me,
I'm the one who keeps having miscarriages."*

*"My baby had a rare genetic issue.
Why would I feel that everything
will work out next time?"*

"This is too big a thing to come back from."

After my first pregnancy loss, I began to question my
assumptions about what my life was going to look like.
I wondered what things I could count on and what
things I could make happen. The life that lay ahead for
me seemed less certain and more risky. I also started
having an ambivalent relationship with the word *hope*.

Merriam-Webster defines hope as "the feeling
of wanting something to happen and thinking that
it could happen; a feeling that something good will
happen or be true."

Hope is something other people usually want us to
feel after our loss. It's an understandable and generally
well-meaning desire. We, however, may struggle with
the concept. It's not like we want to feel hopeless. It's
just that what we are hoping for—to stop feeling so
sad, to have another pregnancy or baby, or to back

up to some pre-loss point in our lives—may feel, and indeed *be*, outside our grasp. We desperately want to feel better but don't know how or whether we'll get there. When someone urges us to be hopeful, it may feel unreasonable and frustrating, as if they're telling us to go swim across the ocean.

In my office, clients have shared many of the well-intended things people have said to them, along with their internal responses to the comments:

"Everything happens for a reason."

> Really? Do you know the reason my baby is dead? Because there can't be a good-enough reason.

"You'll have more kids."

> How could you possibly know that? And even if you are omniscient, do you think this loss will ever become a nonevent?

"Time heals all wounds."

> What kind of time are we talking here? Because I don't know how long I can stand this.

After a loss, we are just not inclined to feel hopeful. Our thoughts are often more along the lines of:

> Everything has gone wrong. I can't imagine things changing for the better.

> I've been on the bad side of the statistics in the past, so hopeful statistics don't mean that much to me.

Hope feels like a setup for being sucker-punched again.

Superstition makes as much sense as anything else right now, and hope might tempt fate.

If I felt hopeful, wouldn't that be a betrayal of the baby?

The big, good thing can't happen. The baby I loved and lost can't come back, so nothing else can really be okay.

With thoughts like these weighing on our mind, how can we possibly feel that something good will happen in the future?

Maybe the obstacle is seeing the "something good in the future" as an outside thing or event that we need to have happen. The quick physical recovery, a more supportive reaction from our family or friends, another pregnancy—these things may or may not happen. And these wishes are pretty emotionally loaded, anyway. Within that framework, hope becomes a tricky proposition.

There is another possibility, however, that is easy to overlook when you're grieving and waiting to feel hopeful. It's that the positive, wished-for thing that's coming is *you*. And you'll show up when you're good and ready.

Most of us are just not wired to sustain misery indefinitely. I also don't think we can (or should try to) snap back out of a loss of someone to whom we were deeply attached. For myself, I know that I couldn't feel better until I had thoroughly explored feeling terrible. It was too big of a loss for me to not feel deeply about it.

But I do remember one day driving a familiar route and wondering how a mountain suddenly appeared in the distance. I hadn't noticed it for the past few weeks when I had been driving on that same highway in the same direction. Something inside me flickered back on for a moment, and the mountain became the focus of my attention. I couldn't figure out how something so beautiful could have ever been invisible. It reminded me that more of my life was coming—and so might be my ability to see it and feel it.

Elizabeth McCracken speaks to this in *An Exact Replica of a Figment of My Imagination*, a memoir of her life carrying and grieving her stillborn son: "Your friends may say, *Time heals all wounds.* No, it doesn't, but eventually you'll feel better. You'll be yourself again. Your child will still be dead. The frivolous parts of your personality, stubborner than you'd imagined, will grow up through the cracks in your soul."[3]

As I look back, I think there was one thing that would have been worth betting on—a good, wonderful thing that I could have hung my hat on—in those early, dark days: the notion that I would eventually be able to see things differently and feel happy again. Not because I have psychological training or because I'm so wonderfully resilient, but because, like most people, I am especially human. And humans are built to wait out the pain and eventually attach to other, good parts of our lives.

Maybe you're ambivalent or resentful about hope. That's fine. You might just want to experiment with the possibility that there is something waiting in you that is bigger than your fears and is respectful of your pain. That part of you won't surface as fast as you would like, and I am truly sorry for that. But even if you can't believe that something in you can and will shift, there may come a day when you glimpse something brighter again. Anyway, it could be worth hoping for.

Chapter 9

GUILT

"No one blames her."
"That never matters,"
said Alec.
"Not when you
blame yourself."

—Cassandra Clare, *City of Lost Souls*

*"Of course it was my fault.
My body couldn't keep her alive."*

*"I was so sick that first trimester,
maybe I wasn't bonding enough
with the baby."*

*"Maybe I should have taken her to the
hospital sooner, or called someone.
I should have known what to do."*

I don't think I've ever met anyone who has experienced a miscarriage, stillbirth, termination due to diagnosis of a fetal abnormality, or infant loss who did not spend some time worrying that she or he had done something to contribute to the loss. And by "some time," I mean usually "quite a bit of time."

I know I did this myself, and I think it's an inevitable part of the grieving process. As a species, we like to make sense of our world. Being pregnant or having a new baby is a huge responsibility. When we are the one carrying the baby or caring for the baby, it's pretty compelling to believe that we have control over what happens on our watch.

I've heard all sorts of things mentioned by women as possible causes of their loss: drinking coffee or having a glass of wine, having sex, riding in an airplane, eating soft cheese or deli meat or nonorganic food, exercising, not exercising, thinking too much or too little about the pregnancy or baby, feeling too positive or not positive enough about the pregnancy or baby.

Although doctors may caution us to avoid some of these things during pregnancy, it is rare to have them actually contribute to a loss. In fact, we all know of women who have been pregnant and delivered relatively healthy babies despite truly extreme circumstances such as addiction or being in the midst of a war or natural disaster. But, although we may hear evidence to the contrary, sometimes it just feels better to blame ourselves than to acknowledge how little control we actually had over something so important.

Pregnancy and childbirth can feel like a time when we are granted special powers. Our body steps up to do amazing things in the way of hormone production, shape shifting, and perceptual superpowers such as a heightened sense of smell and taste. We are tasked with the mind-blowing job of growing a new human and are usually given plenty of advice on how to do it. All of these factors set us up to believe we must be responsible for what happens. If we're not the ones in charge of things going right for our pregnancy or baby, who is?

And then something goes horribly, painfully wrong. Despite all of our strength and intentions, we couldn't stop it from happening. We search the world for a portal to a different reality or a chance for a do-over, and we come up empty. What does that say about us? If it turns out that we aren't Superman, who could make everything safe, are we Lex Luthor, who did something awful to make everything go wrong?

Maybe accepting our part in what happened involves coming to terms with how, despite all of our strong wishes and abilities, when it comes to certain medical realities each one of us is a perpetual Clark Kent with no phone booth in sight. We only ever had a few things under our control, and none of them were enough. If we could have made the world spin backward and saved our baby, we would have. It just wasn't ever an option. Unfortunately, great responsibility doesn't always come with great power (to mix in a Spider-Man reference).

So when your brain prompts you to do the review of what happened and why, try to keep in mind who you're actually dealing with: a loving, heartbroken person. You've already been through a lot, and beating up on yourself isn't helpful or called for. Try speaking to yourself gently, as you would to your best friend if they were going through the same thing.

Think about what you need. Is there any information that might help you to understand—logically or emotionally—what happened? And let me be clear, I'm not recommending extended sessions with Dr. Google. I'm talking more about any big questions that you want to ask your doctor. If so, you may want to try to seek out that information.

If not, or if the information is not that clear or helpful (which, unfortunately, is the case for many of us), work on accepting the story you have with the knowledge that you have. Part of this acceptance is to acknowledge the limited or total lack of control you had over your loss.

As you do your review, don't forget the parts of your story where you went to your prenatal appointments, took your vitamins, and did your best to care for your pregnancy or baby. Don't forget any sweet moments you had while pregnant or with your baby. And definitely remember that your desire to understand what happened comes out of your attachment to someone very dear to you. That ability to attach doesn't come with the ability to fly or change the past, but it's one of the superpowers of an imperfect and loving human.

Chapter 10

ANGER

Don't be afraid to feel as angry or loving as you can.

—Lena Horne

"I just kind of hate people right now."

"The ER doctor was awful to me, and now I can't forgive her."

"I'm mad at God."

One of my favorite descriptions of anger after perinatal loss is from the novel *Luscious Lemon*, by Heather Swain. The narrator, who has just experienced a miscarriage, reluctantly attends a baby shower for a relative:

> "From the living room, I can hear the squeal of women's voices cooing over rubber nipples and car seats. As I peek in on the scene of my slavering aunts and cousins gathered around Trina in full bloom, I wish that I had the technical knowledge to construct a bomb out of a Diaper Genie, Enfamil, and tiny plush toys. I imagine the whole place exploding in one giant poof of confectioner's sugar and me escaping through an open window, shimmying down the drainpipe to freedom."[4]

Anger is an emotion that can make us squirm with discomfort. Many women, in particular, don't get a lot of practice acknowledging or expressing anger. We worry about being rude or mean, or just appearing less than "nice."

In addition to the messages we've received related to gender expectations, there may be racial, cultural, or homophobic stereotypes that play a part in how we feel our anger may be seen by others—and perhaps also in what we are mad about in the first place (for instance, having received substandard medical care as a result of discrimination).

Any of these issues may make us less comfortable expressing anger at a time when it is perfectly natural to be angry. We may also worry about doing anything else that would stress out our support system and, as a result, look at anger as something that should be overcome or managed.

Anger can certainly become a problem, and it can sometimes be useful to examine the feelings underneath an angry reaction. Anger can also be a healthy, appropriate, passing response. But if we shut down our anger at the speed of a game-show contestant trying to be the first to hit the buzzer, we aren't likely to learn anything about ourselves or feel the possible benefits of being angry.

Whether we feel comfortable speaking about it, anger is likely to be a part of our experience after a perinatal loss. As someone once explained to me, the root of the word "bereavement" means "to be robbed." At some point, that feeling that we've been robbed of something valuable hits us—and we're furious about it.

You may be unclear about who has done the robbing and exactly why you're angry, but the feeling is real. Or you may have a clear idea about why you're angry and who you're angry with. Maybe you're mad at someone in the medical field for either their actions or their attitude in caring for you. Maybe you're mad at your higher power or the universe at large. Maybe you're mad at your partner for not grieving the same way as you. Maybe you're mad at your family and friends for doing too much or too little to help you during this time. Maybe you're mad at yourself for not having the power to keep your loss from happening. Maybe it all feels rational, and maybe it doesn't.

If your anger comes out of a perceived wrong related to your loss, you may want to take action in a way that feels constructive. After my first loss, I sent a letter to the medical team thanking a number of the staff who were particularly wonderful. I sent another one to a specific doctor who I felt had been insensitive in his words and behavior, and made my experience more difficult. I tried to be specific and minimize any heat or bitterness as I explained my feedback; I wanted to deliver the message in a way he could hear. I never heard back from him (and didn't expect to), but the action made me feel as if I had done something to stand up for myself and others delivering a stillborn baby.

If you're angry about the behavior of another, forgiveness may also be useful. The purpose is not to be some kind of superior being or do-gooder; it's for your own sense of peace. Psychologist Fred Luskin writes about how forgiveness decreases stress and increases happiness.[5] If your anger at another is taking away from what you want in your life, it may help to read Luskin's work and make your way through the steps to forgiveness.

You may notice some benefits from your anger. Feeling fury can provide energy at a time when you may have very little. It may be the one thing that motivates you to action, even if it's just a difference in how you think something through or move your body on a certain day after a period of despondent inaction. That push of anger may also provide insight as you understand something in a different way. It may just give you a hit of feeling more alive, and you may need that sensation.

Sometimes we find ways to express our anger outside of words. One night when I was facilitating a pregnancy loss group, the group members described various ways of venting their anger, including screaming, breaking things, and, for one woman, going to the rifle range and shooting until exhausted. They all felt relief after their actions. Although a bit embarrassed at the beginning of the discussion, they gathered steam and disclosed more throughout the session. Through their disclosure, they had normalized each other's feelings. They expressed comfort knowing that they were not alone in feeling furious.

This is not necessarily a time when you have to decide if your anger is justified. A good start might be to just notice your feelings. As long as you are not lashing out or otherwise causing injury to yourself or others, anger isn't something that has to be lassoed and managed.

If you are behaving in a way that is hurting yourself or another when you're mad, find some support to learn to work through it in another way. Find a way to express your anger that works for you. You may want to verbalize your feelings to people or write a journal entry, letter, or blog. You can express your anger by making art, hitting a pillow, exercising (as appropriate to your physical condition), or ripping something up.

In the end, as unpleasant as it may be, anger is only an emotion. Like any other emotion, it's waiting for a way to be expressed. It doesn't have to stop you from feeling or being all the other things you are feeling and being. Experiment with not feeding or starving your anger but just acknowledging it. You may learn something about yourself, whether it's that you're able to direct your anger in a useful way or just survive another round of discomfort related to one of our basic human emotions.

Chapter 11

ANXIETY

No one ever told me
that grief felt
so much like fear.

—C. S. Lewis

"Who else am I going to lose?"

*"How can I ever stand being pregnant again?
Or not being pregnant again?"*

*"I keep replaying in my head
all of the terrible things that happened
at the hospital."*

Perinatal bereavement is a startling juxtaposition of birth (actual or anticipated) and death (whether of a baby or dream). It may feel like a dramatic roller coaster ride from an all-time high to a record low in a very short period of time. This extreme drop can leave us quite shaken and scared.

As you probably know firsthand, anxiety comes in a variety of flavors and strengths. It can vary from minor worries to anxiety disorders such as generalized anxiety disorder (exaggerated worries about everyday things) and post-traumatic stress disorder (anxiety reactions following and related to a trauma). Many factors may be affecting your current experience, as well as whether you are a bit of a worrier in general. The details of your loss, including the level of trauma it involved and the meaning your pregnancy or baby has for you, will likely play a part in the level of your anxiety.

And although you might be worried about any number of things, there are certain concerns that commonly raise their head after a reproductive loss.

One is the feeling that the world has suddenly become a precarious place. Previously unimagined things have now happened. What next? You may be waiting for another bad thing to jump out and mess up your life even more. Especially in the early days and weeks after a loss, many people worry about something terrible happening to their partner or to their other current or future children. It's also common to just worry that the recent lousy trajectory of your life will continue and plow you into more pain-inducing experiences.

Thankfully, having a terrible loss does not mean you are now on a course for more of the same. It may be important for you to distinguish between what is happening now and what has taken place in your past. This means noticing that the painful event has already happened. You are having feelings about your loss, but you are not having the exact same experience of loss forever. Despite whatever anxious thoughts are going through your head, this stage of your life is not endless.

In general, if you are looking for ways to address your worries, it helps to start simply. Break things down into whatever size pieces you need. You can practice getting through your life one day at a time, one hour at a time, one minute at a time, or one breath at a time—all fine choices. Whatever size piece you can handle right now, that's all you really need to do.

As you are able, taking small steps out of your comfort zone will help you to let go of fears. This may involve walking halfway down the block after days in the house or waiting another minute to call your partner when he or she is five minutes late. Keep breathing, keep trying, and be patient with yourself.

There are a number of other steps you can take to decrease your anxiety. Many of them are actions you can do on your own such as practicing relaxation exercises, yoga, meditation, or any physical exercise that settles your mind and body. In addition to all the formal suggestions out there for relaxation and stress management, don't forget the power of a good deep breath or a walk in nature.

Anxiety usually involves some negative self-talk— those things that you say to yourself that raise your blood pressure, for example, "I'm never going to be free of this pain. I don't think I can stand it." You may need to find gentle ways to speak to yourself about what you're feeling. Kinder self-talk might sound like: "I'm grieving a baby I loved, and my life is really hard right now, but I will get through this." It can also be reassuring to discuss your concerns with people in your support system, whether friends, family, or a grief group (in person or online).

Self-compassion is an important ingredient to this. Being compassionate with yourself means approaching yourself with a stance of kindness, patience, and gentleness. I can't think of a better time than now to make a concerted effort to respect yourself in this way. The opposite—bullying yourself for being anxious— can be an old and compelling script for many of us, but it's not a very useful one. Become a compassionate companion to yourself and show up for the part of you that is scared and trying to find the way.

Chapter 12

LONELINESS

Loneliness is proof
that your innate search
for connection is intact.

—Martha Beck

"With the baby gone,
I just feel cold and empty inside."

"I've never felt more alone."

"I was so connected to everyone before the loss.
Now I don't feel connected to anyone."

At the Monterey Bay Aquarium, there is an exhibit called the Kelp Forest. Standing twenty-eight feet tall and spanning an enormous room, it's a glass tank that houses an underwater ecosystem. The diffused light from above reveals a somewhat out-of-focus background of variegated blues and greens with streaks of yellow and brown plant life. Sharks, octopuses, sardines, bright orange garibaldi, and a host of other bay creatures swim past giant strands of swaying kelp that reach up from the bottom of the tank. The exhibit provides a close-up view of another world held steadfast behind the glass.

Sometimes life after loss reminds me of visiting the Kelp Forest with the missing someone on the other side of the glass. We can catch glimpses of them through the lens of memory, dreams, or other ways we may find to connect. We can consider their beauty and mystery, but there is an ongoing separation that is unmistakable and unchangeable.

It can feel pretty damn lonely.

After the fire trucks that responded to our collective baby losses turned off their lights and drove away, a painful silence may have followed. The previous relationship we had been feeling with our child or child-to-be was drastically altered or stilled. And instead of our baby, an absence has come to live with us.

Loneliness in general can be described in many ways: sadness and longing for company, or feeling cut off from others, remote, unseen, unwanted, or unneeded. The loneliness of baby loss can be all of the above, with an added physical emptiness and yearning since—either in our bodies when pregnant or in our arms after birth—the baby was so a part of us. There is an intense desire for reconnection. We may hear echoes of all the different versions of our life we wish were happening instead of this one. Loneliness can be acute or chronic, pretty bearable or an intense middle-of-the-night kind of agony.

It can also be useful.

In the loneliness of missing our babies, it may feel as if we are the ones who are lost. Like other experiences of being lost, though, loneliness gives us a different point of view. We may feel more raw, more open. We may feel all of our edges, acutely aware of what is left of ourselves when everything else falls away.

I'm not recommending an extended stay in this place; I'm just saying that short visits don't have to be feared. Noticing your loneliness without jumping up to change your experience allows you to practice tolerating discomfort. You get to practice being aware of your feelings and bearing them as they arrive and pass, without the distractions and interruptions of other people's presence and energy. You may be able to tolerate your feelings alone for just a few short moments at a time, but it is empowering to know that you can do it.

Being lonely also gives you the opportunity to show up for yourself. This means breaking out the self-care by speaking kindly to yourself ("I'm hurting and missing my baby, and I will get through this moment"), reviewing and addressing your basic needs (eating, sleeping, being safe), or hitting your list of comforting activities (meditating, reading, exercise, taking a bath, etc.).

When you're lonely, you're likely to seek relief by looking outside yourself. Although there is much to be said for reaching out and getting support during this time, it may not be the first thing you need—and it won't be the only thing you need. Just as your relationship to your baby was unique, so is your loss. That doesn't mean that others can't empathize and connect with you in lots of important ways; they can, and you will need them to do so. But there is a part that is always yours to carry alone, and it's valuable to practice doing that.

Relationships may look different viewed from a distance. Not getting what you want from others for a given time can help you to clarify those needs and wants. Your needs may be met well by the people in your life now, or you might notice that some of your current priorities for a relationship mean that you want to expand your world. You might also notice a greater need for boundaries or other changes that you wish to make to your relationships.

Sitting with loneliness can lead to new and important experiences. Feeling lonely and not rushing to change the feeling may lead you to tolerating other feelings and practicing how to sit with them as they come and go. Noticing your loneliness can also inspire you to do more to take care of yourself, something that most of us need to keep practicing. It may also give you the space to reflect on what is most important to you in your changed life, including any shifting priorities regarding what you want from your relationships.

Sometimes we need to visit a place of separation to truly understand what we're seeking from ourselves and others.

Chapter 13
SELF-ESTEEM

We are not broken,
we are just
unfinished.

—Dawna Markova

"I feel like I've been held back a grade in school."

"Why is it so easy
for everyone except me
to have a baby?"

"I just feel like a loser."

Losing a baby can make us feel as if we have failed in some huge way and that our loss reveals some underlying inadequacy on our part. Our sense of the world and ourselves might be a bit unsteady, making us less sure of ourselves and our abilities. If we're looking for ways that we don't measure up, we can surely find them everywhere.

Maybe our siblings are the ones who had kids and made our parents into grandparents and get to have the holiday card that features a baby, while our arms are still empty. Or maybe suddenly all of social media seems to be filled with birth announcements that "everyone's healthy and doing well" after we lost a baby who was not healthy or developing normally. Or we ache when we note that the couple who moved into our neighborhood with the nice schools at the same time we did now has a child who will go to them, while our child is gone.

Although the loss you experienced was probably totally out of your hands, it is amazing how inadequate you may feel in the wake of your crisis. If your loss involved a physical challenge, like "incompetent cervix" (which, I hope we can all agree, is a condition in need of a new name), it can be difficult not to conclude that *you* are incompetent.

However, your reproductive problems do not define you, and your unsteadiness will not last forever. That said, when you could not complete a pregnancy or keep your baby healthy and alive, it can be hard to separate that physical inability from a sense of personal failure.

Just living after a shocking loss can make you feel less secure in general. The world looks different, and people may be treating you quite differently. If people seem nervous around you, or if you perceive them as treating you with pity, it can highlight feelings of inadequacy. This dynamic can start a negative loop in which you think that others see you as lesser, and you react to that assumed judgment.

Moving through the world with a sense of insecurity about your reproductive future may color other parts of your life. At work, you may notice that your lower sense of self-worth is taking a toll. It may be a harder time to take on something new, or you may be quick to feel defeated in a project. Unconsciously, you may overgeneralize a perceived failure in one area of life to all other areas of life.

Although this might be obvious to you during a less-stressful time, you may need a reminder that there is a difference between being someone who needs extra time and help because of a medical or emotional condition, and being someone who has lost their abilities or their value to society. Needing more right now does not mean that this is your new permanent status. It may help to remember that everyone goes through tough times—whether it is a financial setback, a medical crisis, or an unexpected and heartbreaking loss.

As you take your first tentative steps in the world, don't forget to acknowledge small accomplishments and give yourself credit. Whether you were able to make it through a work call without crying, attend your first support group, or make dinner for the first time since your loss, let yourself highlight the progress. These activities may have been routine in the past and will be again in the future, but, right now, you deserve a pat on the back for such steps. Having enough bandwidth to attend to your partner counts as something positive too, since doing so reminds you that you have something to give, even if it's hard.

So, in this moment, if you feel fragile, unsettled, or a bit wobbly in the world—good to know. I'm glad you can acknowledge it. That's where you are today. There is probably an excellent reason for your current state, and I can imagine the relief you'll feel when you get to a better place. For now, you may need to make some temporary changes, like adjusting your work schedule or committing to extra self-care. But it would be unfair (not to mention unhelpful) to base your self-worth on your misfortune or to mistake your healing time for weakness. You may have lost a great deal, but you have not lost what is good or worthwhile about yourself.

Imagine how you might speak to a friend who was in your shoes. Imagine how important it might be to treat her respectfully and thoughtfully. Just as you might want to be an especially good friend to her, you can be a better friend to yourself by noticing with compassion what the real challenges and feelings are, and showing up for yourself in whatever way you are able to manage at this moment. Treating yourself with the kindness you deserve is a sign of self-respect, and it's also a great step toward feeling better.

Chapter 14

COMPARISONS

No one's life ever goes
as they planned.
That truth alone
should bring a sense of
relief to everyone.

—Andrena Sawyer

"At least I got to hold my baby."

*"Her loss was later than mine,
so it was much worse."*

*"I don't have a partner—
no one can understand
what I'm going through."*

It is simply a human tendency to compare ourselves and our struggles to others. For those of us grieving babies, this impulse can be one of the primary ways we try to orient ourselves and comfort ourselves while walking around this new, unexplored planet. We compare how far along we were in the pregnancy or how old our baby was, what we have experienced emotionally and physically, and how we are coping. I did this the day I lost my baby seventeen years ago, and I do this today as I write these words. It is both the most normal thing in the world and a potentially damaging bit of thinking.

Sometimes the comparison may bring us relief. I've heard women say things like "At least I didn't have to make any decisions about ending my baby's life" or "It would have been so much harder if I had been further along" or "At least I got to see my baby." It may give us a sense of solace that our loss is not the very worst experience we can imagine or have heard about. It may help us tolerate our own pain to acknowledge that someone somewhere is surviving an even worse fate.

Unfortunately, comparing ourselves to others can also hurt us. This is because it's never quite a fair comparison between our rich, complicated lives and circumstances and those of another. Especially when the reality is that we may not really know that much about someone else's experience. When we compare ourselves to others without really knowing what it is like to be them, we're always making part of it up—and usually feeling bad about what we believe. Thinking someone else is doing grief better, or is more deserving of compassion, or isn't suffering as badly as us probably isn't doing much to make us feel steadier or better about ourselves in this time of crisis.

These comparisons may also create distance between people who would otherwise be in a great place to support each other. In leading pregnancy loss groups for women, I've had an up-close picture of the different ways we use comparisons between ourselves and others in processing our grief.

Some of the women in these groups had recurrent early miscarriages, and some had later losses (after twenty or more weeks' gestation). A few of the women had delivered babies so premature that they lived only minutes or hours. Some of the women had living children prior to their loss, while others did not. Some had previous experiences with abortion or adoption, which affected how they perceived their current perinatal loss. A few had lost multiples, and most had been carrying one baby. Some of the women had known infertility issues, while others had every reason to expect that they could easily conceive again. Most of the women had partners, but some did not. Most women were straight; some were gay or bisexual. Some of the women had severe physical or emotional trauma associated with their losses. A number of the women had losses caused by factors (such as physical limitations or genetic issues) that would make future pregnancies potentially higher risk or more likely to result in a baby with severe medical problems. Some had subsequent pregnancies while in the group, and some did not.

All of these differences mattered or had the potential to matter to any given group member at any given time. It periodically made the group very challenging. As people noticed a difference that they thought made someone else's experience better or worse, more or less hopeful, or more or less survivable, feelings of envy, guilt, and isolation were often expressed. The very human focus on differences sometimes put up temporary fences separating people who, in that moment, could otherwise have been helpful to each other.

Yet, in spite of their differences, the group members shared a simple bond: grieving a baby (or babies) to whom they were attached. In some ways, a powerful link was created when a woman could feel that another in her group experienced a similar type of loss. To share the heartbreak of what it had been like to get the best news of one's life, only to have hopes crushed with the onset of early bleeding, formed a bond. Similarly, when someone had lost a baby most of the way through a pregnancy, meeting another person who was surviving a similar version of heartbreak could be reassuring.

But as they got to know one another, it became clear that the details of any particular loss was not what would make or break the bonds between them. The women all grieved someone for whom they had feelings of love and about whom they had been excited, someone for whom they were willing to try rearranging their lives, someone so small and yet so big that the loss had left them rearranged. The attachment and loss had carved out a space inside them, and they were somehow connected to one another through those spaces.

And that made them people of the same planet. They could understand each other's language and customs, even if they were not immediate relatives. These women shared many of the same feelings of sadness, anger, guilt, confusion, envy, and anxiety. Their self-esteem and identity had taken a beating because they had started out on the road of pregnancy and dropped off the map before reaching their destination: the place where they had a living baby.

They inhabited a planet where life without their baby was hard, sometimes seemingly impossible. They were in a place where life meant living in a body that was missing someone or something, with hearts that were split open, and where minimal tangible evidence of what was lost remained. Seeing the shared pain opened them up to feeling compassion for each other, which often helped them to have more compassion for themselves. It gave them something to recognize, feel, and tolerate together.

When comparing our losses, we are isolating ourselves. Differences are real, but they may not be the most useful thing to focus on. When you are vulnerable and in pain, it may help to notice who can cross any bridges that lie between you, and be with you where you are. The connection may be formed by a shared life experience that shaped something inside you in a similar way, or it may be the empathy and skill that enables another to come find you where you are. Try to notice who is emotionally available to you. Let that person (or people) help you by being in this with you.

Chapter 15

FIRST MOVES

The Guide says
there is an art to flying...
or rather a knack.
The knack lies in
learning how to throw
yourself at the ground
and miss.

—Douglas Adams, *Life, the Universe,
and Everything*

*"I'm not really getting out of the house
these days, but I sometimes talk to my mom
on the phone."*

*"We went out to dinner and I started crying
after a couple with a baby was seated
next to us."*

*"I tried going to a friend's party. It was so
weird trying to pretend anything in my world
was sort of okay. I had to leave."*

My partner is a pilot, and he has tried, repeatedly and unsuccessfully, to teach me the physics of flying. So far there is only one fact that has really stayed with me. It's this: after we have put fuel in the plane, ensured all the parts are working, buckled in, started the propeller, communicated with the tower, moved the throttle, flicked lots of switches, and gone skittering down the runway in that wonderful, jerky fashion of small planes—after all of the steps and effort are made by the pilot to leave the solid surface of the earth—it is the air flowing over the wings that pulls the plane off the ground.

This piece of knowledge is remarkably unhelpful in moving me toward my goal of being able to land the airplane in an emergency, but it does help me make sense of some other things. The pilot and I have had to scrap plans due to weather, mechanical problems, and previously reserved airspace (usually due to VIP events on our desired route). Doing all that we can do may lead to success or being thwarted; there are forces beyond us that support us or work against us in a particular effort. Learning when to push on and when to call it are part of the deal, and sometimes we can't know until the last minute if our efforts were in vain.

After losing our babies, returning to the smallest tasks of daily living can feel colossal, but, at some point, we are ready to take a step into the world. Okay, maybe we aren't really *ready* for anything, but whether it is a first post-loss shower or an attempt to make a sandwich, we will start to make some small moves. These tasks may feel all wrong, because everything is wrong without our baby, but we still try. Even if it feels like we are dragging around an unrecognizable self, it's a move, and it matters.

The initial shock of loss can make small mental steps surprisingly easy. Sometimes we are astonishingly clear in the first hours or even days after our loss. We make the calls to tie up our leave from work or to make sure someone will be walking the dog. But some of us never have that initial clarity, and, even if we do, it eventually wears off and turns to numbness that makes for fuzzier thinking.

The headline of the day, every day, for some time might be that your baby is gone. The blinking, bold fact is rightfully bigger than others in your brain. That's not doing it wrong; that's processing your reality. There will be space for other headlines farther down the road. But if you find yourself with less room for other thoughts and plans right now, it is respectful to adjust your life to that place.

That might mean adjusting expectations about work and other responsibilities. Even if you can make yourself "power through," it's worth considering that pushing yourself when your internal resources are depleted might make it harder in the long run. Grief saps your time and energy, and you may do better if you act accordingly. As tempting as it might be to think you will be more comfortable or healthy if you return quickly to your normal schedule and responsibilities, you may end up internally lost, with a mismatch between where you are and where you are pretending to be.

Physical moves can be another challenge. Although I often say that physical exercise, as appropriate to your current condition, can be helpful, that "current condition" part can be tricky to assess. In my case, I convinced myself shortly after my first loss that I was ready to do my usual hiking loop. Although I was able to drag myself through it, I ended up in the ER that night due to excessive bleeding caused by overexertion. Being back at the hospital where I had just delivered was so not what I wanted in that moment. It was physically and emotionally tough to get through. I wish I had tuned in to where my body was and avoided that extra suffering.

And at some point, your heart will be on the move too. Preoccupation with your baby and your loss is normal, and it may feel like a way to connect to and show love for the one you have lost. You may fear that attaching to anyone or anything else, whether it's another baby or just another person or thing you love in the world, is wrong.

Fortunately, love isn't an endangered resource, no matter what your anxiety is telling you. It's not an either/or choice, as you live on after your baby or pregnancy is gone. When your heart is ready to care for something or someone else, there will be room.

When we're making a move in the mental, physical, or emotional realm after perinatal loss, we will have stops, starts, and missteps. As always, life is about showing up and trying. We will have learning curves and fall on our faces sometimes. And it won't be all up to us. We are trying to navigate a new situation with a changed self, and there are many different factors at work. Our body may not cooperate, our support system may fail us, and financial, political, and social aspects of our world may make things harder.

Living after baby loss, like living the rest of life, is about reaching for the next thing in front of us, no matter how small. It just tends to be a hell of a lot harder than most of the other chapters we've lived. We can only try to be there in the right position, moving at the right speed, and holding on tight, waiting for the lift created by our forward momentum.

Chapter 16

THE GRIEVING COUPLE

We have so little faith in
the ebb and flow of life,
of love, of relationships.
We leap at the flow of
the tide and resist in
terror its ebb.

—Anne Morrow Lindbergh

"I don't think my wife should wallow in it and be so sad all the time. I mean, there's nothing we can do about it, so let's move on."

"Sometimes I wonder if he misses her or understands how I feel about our baby. I wonder if I've lost him too."

"She acts like everything is fine and we just need to get pregnant again. Does she think that will make it all better?"

Sharing a pregnancy or baby is, in itself, a form of intimacy. A baby is of us and of our relationship in a primary way. Babies are most commonly biologically connected to us. When that is not the case, the road to pregnancy or adoption is likely to have been a long one that included great effort, planning, and intention. Going through a pregnancy or having a baby with a partner tends to be a time that stands apart from the rest of our time together. We may have higher highs, lower lows, and scarier scares together.

It is a time of greater interdependence and need as the couple undertakes a journey together to bring a new person into the world. Even if other pregnancies have come before or are expected in the future, this time is a bit different. The wishes, fears, expectations, and memories of a specific pregnancy are exactly that: specific to that pregnancy and special in their own ways.

And after baby loss? That experience is shared too, but two partners are never affected in the exact same way. The fallout is never quite evenly distributed. Although so much can be and usually is shared, one person is likely to have been more attached to the baby or more ambivalent about the pregnancy or more physically affected by the loss than the other.

However, it's not necessarily that one partner feels more or less overall; it's more that the jagged edges of the broken place are just not exactly the same for each person. Those fractured places may be similar, perhaps just as painful, but different.

Perinatal loss is a huge challenge for any couple to face. When we took vows to stand by our partner for better or for worse, we didn't picture *this*. When we saw that second line on the pregnancy test or heard the excited words from our mate, we had no idea that it would end this way. But, somehow, this is the bus we ended up on and this is the ride we are taking, individually and together.

Sometimes we may find our partner extremely comforting to us during a moment of intense grief. After all, he or she is likely the person to whom we feel closest and with whom we shared most of the baby experience. Our partner may be great at knowing what we need and being able to provide it much of the time. In fact, many people say they felt closer than ever to their partner after a perinatal loss.

But all of us, in the midst of our own imperfections, pain, and sense of overwhelm, run the risk of adding to our partner's suffering at some point. Even in the strongest relationships, there are likely to be moments (sometimes many) of disappointment or anger after our loss. We may experience these upsets as passing challenges or big crises that scare us and cause us to worry that, on top of everything else, we may lose our relationship too.

Sometimes partners injure each other because they don't know how to react in the midst of this type of life event. After all, whoever took the prep course on how to lose a baby? When new to grief, or to this type of grief, many of us hold assumptions about what we or our partner should be feeling or doing, and then are intolerant when the expectations are not met. It may be a husband who thinks his wife is "making too much" over an early miscarriage. It may be a woman who is angry and hurt that her partner does not want to see pictures of their stillborn son. The difficulty accepting each other may be spoken aloud or just implied, leading to distance and pain for the couple.

Injury can also occur simply due to depleted resources. When we are maxed out by sadness and fatigue (and grief *is* exhausting), it is harder to do the work of reaching out and connecting with our partner. I am not the first to note that grief tends to be a rather self-absorbing experience, and we may notice ourselves turned inward much of the time. It can be easy to look at the distance between us and our beloved and worry that we are no longer on the same side.

Of course, these issues just scratch the surface of what can arise in a couple's life after the loss of a baby, but they are the ones that are familiar to most of us who have been in this situation.

Rather than jumping to conclusions about your own or your partner's reaction to the loss, try to first notice what you're feeling and thinking. Be curious about what has come up for you in terms of beliefs about what you or your partner should be doing. Consider that these assumptions may stem from cultural, gender, or personality influences as well as your own history of loss. Acknowledge and take responsibility for your own bias, remembering that we all have them.

Unless your partner is acting in a way that you think is dangerous, try to respect that he or she is having an experience different from yours and is entitled to be in that place. If you can suspend judgments about right or wrong, and work on accepting and acknowledging that each of you is grieving differently, it can neutralize some of the anxiety and the hurtful reactions that follow. The truth is, however close or similar you and your partner may be, the two of you are different people who had different experiences with the pregnancy or baby, as well as the circumstances of the loss. As a result, you can't possibly have the exact same grief experience.

Although it's important to allow for the space inherent in holding different views and feelings, it's also important to find ways to meet and connect. This may be far easier in some moments than others, and that's okay. Being open to the idea will help you to notice opportunities. Remember that both of you are going through a painful and confusing time. You are also both adjusting to a big change in the story of your lives together, and you may be unsure of how the two of you will be in this new chapter.

You may want to be transparent about your intention to try to connect. Some couples make time at the end of the day to briefly check in to say how they are each feeling and what they need. Other couples work together on a project such as planning a memorial or making something together to honor their baby. It may be particularly helpful to acknowledge difficult feelings about the loss to your loved one. I've heard many people say that they would much rather have their partners disclose their sadness or fear than to "be strong" for them.

Pain and distance in our primary relationship can feel like another layer of loss. Living in this time of grief challenges us in ways we may never have anticipated. It is also a time when couples can grow as they learn how to support themselves and each other in the midst of this crisis.

Chapter 17

SEX

After you experience
the loss of a loved one,
a solid boundary
suddenly stands before
you. It feels as though
you've hit a hard wall,
and you need to find
some softness in your life.
Death is the breaking of
a connection, while sex
can be the establishment
of one.

—Elizabeth Kübler-Ross

"Since we lost our baby, I just don't want to be touched in that way."

"We've been dealing with infertility and miscarriages for so long, sex has a whole different association for me now. There's nothing sexy about it."

"I actually feel more interested in sex right now. Is that normal?"

The most loaded of three-letter words, "sex" can mean so many things to us: comfort, excitement, pleasure, intimacy, fun, freedom, and an affirmation of life. It may feel like a physical need at times and a spiritual event at others. It can feel like one of the best parts of life and the epitome of an expression of love between us and our partner.

Unfortunately, after baby loss, it can also mean some other things.

One is physical pain for the partner who carried the baby. This may be related to a vaginal delivery, C-section, or termination procedure; sore breasts due to lactation; or another medical issue. Although this should be temporary, it can feel especially distressing or confusing to have a trigger that links something special between you and your partner to the physical discomfort associated with your baby who is not with you.

Of course, it can also mean emotional pain because you're grieving and lots of things are emotionally painful right now. If you are in an opposite-sex relationship, sex can feel like a distressing reminder of how the two of you made a baby who can't be here with you. Having to use birth control during the time you expected to be pregnant can feel both weird and sad. If you have had fertility challenges, it may remind you of another chapter of your reproductive history that has been painful.

You may also be feeling confused about what sex means now. Are you "back to normal"? Trying again? You may be putting pressure on yourself to understand and decide things that cannot yet be understood or decided.

It is also normal, yet miserable, to feel guilty about doing something enjoyable. You may feel like it is a betrayal of your baby to do something physically pleasurable. This is often part of the fallout of grieving. You may feel like you are in and out of your body, and in and out of living.

It's also possible that sex is especially appealing because you need to feel comforted, connected, alive, or not alone, and sex is providing that for you. On the other hand, sex may feel impossible because you don't feel comfortable in your body, because you don't feel playful, because you don't feel safe or sexy. In your world, right now, you can't stand to be any more vulnerable, and sex calls for making yourself vulnerable. Your delivery was traumatic and now sex triggers anxiety. You're too exhausted, you're too preoccupied—there's a massive number of other reasons for not wanting to have sex.

Wherever you and your partner might be regarding sex, you likely have some significant differences. You both are hurting from your loss and coping in different ways. In addition, you lost some things as a pair, such as your identity as an expecting couple or parents of a new baby, along with your dreams of where that path would take you. You are both changed by your loss, and part of what you shared is gone.

Your bedroom can feel like a new world that you have to learn to navigate both individually and together. Sex may seem intimidating or unappealing for some time because of the feelings of acute grief and the need to relearn your connection with each other. The changed landscape of the bedroom can feel like a huge secondary loss, but it is probably a short-lived one and one you can work on.

If your sexual experience with your partner feels out of sync, it may help to remember that the dissonance is more likely a phase of your relationship than a permanent change. You may need to start slowly because you're not exactly the same as you were before your loss, and it's unlikely that your sexual self will be immediately back online. Having that in mind and managing expectations can help you and your partner give each other the time you need.

One place you can start is to communicate what your needs are and what sex means to you right now—things that might be quite different than they have been in the past or will be in the future. Remember that communication is itself a form of intimacy: it helps you to know each other better and offers opportunities to connect.

Physical intimacy may feel comforting to one of you and not so much to the other. It doesn't make one of you wrong; it may just take some time to bridge the gap. In *The Five Love Languages: How to Express Heartfelt Commitment to Your Mate*, Gary Chapman popularized the idea that people have their love tank filled by different means, which he categorized into physical intimacy, quality time, acts of service, gifts, or words of affirmation.[6] As a general concept, this can be helpful to consider when you and your partner seem to express and feel love or intimacy in different ways.

You can broaden your definition of intimacy by discussing what makes you feel close, connected, or turned on, and considering new possibilities. Even after you have communicated about your differences and worked on accepting them, there may be ways to expand what feels connecting to each of you. For example, in the realm of physical intimacy, if sexual intercourse is not the right thing for one or both of you right now, you might want to experiment with holding hands or massage as a starting point.

You can also make a plan to spend time alone together and consider how you would like to use it. Walking, talking, crying, or sitting together can all be healing and intimate experiences.

You may want to learn about sensate focus, a technique developed by William H. Masters and Virginia E. Johnson for couples experiencing a variety of sexual challenges.[7] It involves a series of steps that focus on touch, initially nonsexual, to explore what is pleasurable. Sensate focus provides a structured and nonthreatening way to revisit a sexual connection that has been challenged for any reason. For couples who have been through baby loss, the technique may take some of the pressure and triggers away from sex by shifting the focus to a slow, physical exploration.

The intimacy of sexual expression between partners is related to the intimacy of pregnancy and having a baby. Losing a baby can turn the world upside down for a couple in so many ways, including their sex life. By looking at your individual reactions to physical intimacy, noticing what is happening between you and your partner, and experimenting with ways to reconnect, the two of you can return to a closer emotional and physical relationship.

Chapter 18

TRYING AGAIN

I am half agony,
half hope.

—Jane Austen, *Persuasion*

"Should we try again?"

"I'm afraid that it's the only way I'll feel better."

"What if we lose another one?"

I always feel a bit startled when I read an article or book on loss that recommends that we not make any major life decisions while we're grieving. How might that work with baby loss? It's not like pregnancy or infant loss comes with an express ticket through grief or an extension on the childbearing window. And that baby longing probably isn't going anywhere, either.

But I understand where those authors are coming from when they voice this concern. Of course, there's a difference between jumping to a decision immediately after a loss and waiting some weeks, months, or longer. Waiting allows us to metabolize our feelings, at least part way. That's important, and I recommend giving ourselves whatever time and space we can. However, my experience is that the feelings accompanying our loss will still be actively with us when other factors compel us to make a decision about trying for another baby.

Our brain on grief may not be the best mindset for choosing what neighborhood to move to or what kind of car we'll need for the next ten years. In the midst of grieving our baby, it may not seem possible to do a good job of making decisions that require us to weigh facts and anticipate the needs and desires of our future self. Yet, somehow, that's exactly what we do. We have to and we do.

I wish I had a road map to give you so that you could know where your destination is and feel assured that you will get there. You definitely deserve such a thing—a guide through the decision about whether and how to try again when you are heartbroken and know that pregnancy does not always equal living baby, and that sometimes things can go so terribly wrong. If I had such a map, I would offer it to you. But some of the places we visit in life don't lend themselves to mapping. The terrain will be different for each of us and may even vary for us individually at different times. For that reason, this walk is less a determined march and more a humble exploration.

That said, you are traveling a road with many other people ahead of you and alongside you. Some things are known. There are some landmarks, and some places to pause.

A first stop is often where you spend some time trying to understand how likely it is that whatever version of pain and bad luck struck before will strike again. This may be a short visit or a long layover.

Medical appointments, tests, procedures, or research might all be needed or desired. And then there will be a time to stop doing those things and get back en route, remembering that you can google your heart out and still never get the specific answer to the question *What will happen if I try again?*

Less clear is the part of the journey where you figure out what you are up for emotionally. Trying for a baby is always a leap of faith. When your previous leap landed you facedown at the bottom of a gully, it makes sense to evaluate whether you are up for trying again. The stretch of road where you examine your feelings is one you may travel in fits and starts, and it will probably take a lot out of you. It's also one that deserves your attention.

It may take many attempts to reach the crossroads where at last you make your choice. The decision itself may look familiar, or it may be brand new. Your heart may be clearly pulling strong toward trying for another baby. As scary as the feeling might be, it may fill you with hope. It may feel healing. The question at this point becomes how best to take care of yourself while you move in this direction. Remember, regardless of how things turn out, another pregnancy or baby would absolutely be a different one than the one that came before.

You may also decide to take another path besides the one you took in the past, maybe trying assisted reproduction or family building through adoption. Trying in a new way requires an investment of time and learning—and, unfortunately, a significant amount of money—but it may be the way to go for medical or emotional reasons. For some people, taking a new approach has the extra benefit of drawing a sharp line between the next experience and the previous one. That said, any direction would be an adjustment from the path you were on with your previous pregnancy or baby.

That brings us to the question of when. You may feel that you want to try again as soon as possible. You may realize that you need to wait a while. You are likely aware of some time sensitivity and that any direction, even standing still, is at some point a decision.

Finally, for all kinds of reasons, you may feel that your best decision is to remain child-free or without more living children than you already have. This could be a matter of age or finances; it could come from the understanding that this path can lead you to a happy and meaningful life. Finding others who have done the same thing may help. Acceptance and enjoyment of the life you have can't be forced, but it can be found.

The decision of whether to try again for a baby after perinatal loss tends to come down to a combination of fact finding and soul searching in the midst of what can be debilitating pain. The question may stop you in your tracks with fear or confusion, but it can also wake you up with need and hope. After baby loss you are keenly aware that you have not been and will not be offered a risk-free life. You are not calling all the shots. But the combination of hope and intention is powerful. It contains in itself some meaning and beauty. At the end of your path, it's your moment to pick your dandelions, take a deep breath, and blow.

Chapter 19

TALKING ABOUT IT

If we knew each other's
secrets, what comforts
we should find.

—John Churton Collins

*"Sometimes I want to talk,
but there's no one I want to talk to."*

"I don't even have the words right now."

*"I want people to know about him,
but I worry what people will think of me."*

Years ago, sometime after I became an adult but before
I had experienced much in the way of loss, I had a
doctor's appointment with someone who was covering
for my regular provider. I wasn't there for anything
urgent, and I don't remember many details about the
visit. I do, however, remember one thing very clearly:
in the midst of the chitchat between me and this
fortyish physician, she mentioned something sweet
that her daughter had done. The doctor gently added,
"She's passed away since then." After this comment,
she continued to talk and move through the rest of the
appointment in a calm, warm, and professional manner.

I'd like to tell you that I said something kind,
respectful, and openhearted in response, but I
highly doubt it. I just remember being floored by
the mention of a dead child. I felt stunned, sad, and
awkward. It probably showed. It was hard for me
to imagine that this woman had gotten up that day,

had breakfast, dressed for work, and was keeping a not-all-that-consequential appointment with me, all while her daughter was dead. It also startled me that she could talk about her daughter in such a natural and beautiful way. After all these years, I still think about it. It was a challenging, memorable, and helpful moment for me.

"Talk about it." It's advice often given to the bereaved. We probably all have ideas as to why this is a good idea. It can be a relief to share feelings instead of having them bottled up inside. Talking about the loss can also be a way to connect to others and to feel less alone. Better talking than acting out through overworking, drinking, or drugs, right?

It may also be an important way for us to take another look at ourselves and acknowledge who and where we are.

In the pregnancy loss group I used to facilitate, whenever a new member joined, each member, beginning with those who had been in the group for a while, would tell their baby loss story in whatever level of detail they wished. Sometimes this brought up anxiety for people as they anticipated what it might feel like to revisit the events that they experienced so acutely painfully. There were usually tears and sometimes trembling voices.

However, as time went on and people retold their stories, they would often comment on how their stories changed as they revisited and shared them. There were still tears and sometimes trembling voices. But there were also different details noted as more or less important, and there were also changes in emotional resonance. Over time, group members seemed to hold their loss less as a "hot potato" or a cutoff portion of their lives and more as an integrated part of their history.

That single comment made by someone I met only once helped me, because it challenged the way I thought about grief and what it must be like to lose someone so critical to one's identity and happiness. It felt like a significant communique from one woman's experience in the field of grief. The doctor helped me consider the possibility that a person can live with a profound absence in her heart without having her heart close down entirely. She showed me an example of a person respecting her own grief, her lost child, and her ongoing life.

Of course, I don't know what the physician's mention of her daughter and her loss did for her. But that one encounter made me think that a continuing conversation about one's loss may be the way to go. The conversation may be a lot of monologues

interspersed with dialogues. The audience may
be one or larger. The conversation may have many
twists, turns, and moods to it. It may make people
uncomfortable. It may help them immensely. It may do
both. It may help connect some dots and fill in some
colors to help others understand us. It may give us a
clearer view of ourselves.

Chapter 20

TWO SIDES OF OUR STORY

We can't live in the light all of the time. You have to take whatever light you can hold into the dark with you.

—Libba Bray, *A Great and Terrible Beauty*

*"I was just starting to feel okay,
and then today I got hit by another wave
of feeling awful."*

*"How can I laugh?
I lost what mattered most to me."*

*"I go to work and try to forget
that I was pregnant two weeks ago,
then I go home and cry."*

I once spent a few days at an off-the-grid hot springs establishment. On my first trip to the outdoor bathrooms, I smiled as I saw that they were labeled "yin" and "yang." I'm used to figuring out that I'm supposed to head for doors marked "Damas" or "Cowgirls," but this was a nice twist on the concept. It turns out that sometimes a trip to the toilet in a beautiful and quirky location is a good opportunity to consider the relationship between the opposing sides of life.

In Chinese philosophy, yin and yang describes how opposite or contrary forces are actually complementary, interconnected, and interdependent in the natural world, and how they give rise to each other as they interrelate to one another. Sometimes people talk about the two sides as male and female, fire and water, passive and active, moon and sun, and so on. The yin-yang symbol is divided in halves of contrasting colors, yet each half has a dot of the opposite color in it, reminding us that each side contains a bit of the other element.

The experience of expecting or having a baby and then losing that baby tends to give us a dizzying trip to both the light and dark sides of life. It's often a steep drop from one extreme to the other: joy/ sadness, expecting/disbelief, hopeful/hopeless, assured/anxious, expansive/contracted, connecting/ detaching, full/empty, beginning/ending. Certainly none of these feelings are unique to losing a baby. But babies tend to bring out our strongest and most tender feelings, and the abrupt and dramatic shift of attaching to them and losing them is particularly stunning.

The outlier moments in our life—those that are bigger, whether bright or dark—demand notice. They take our energy and attention, and form landmarks in our memory. The two halves of the spinning, messy embrace we see in the yin-yang symbol remind me of times when I have felt the opposing sides of my own life experience.

I have a memory of being five months pregnant on an Easter Sunday. I was lying on a lounge chair in the backyard of my then-home, feeling the sunshine on my skin and the movements of my baby inside me. At that moment everything felt connected and right.

I have memories of being in the hospital a couple of weeks later and feeling that I was losing more than I could handle. People mentioned how beautiful the weather was outside, and I remember thinking that they must be living on another planet. I wondered if anything could feel okay again.

At the time, the two experiences seemed worlds apart. As I think about this now, it seems clear that it was two sides of my loving and losing someone dear to me. The memories now are held as interrelated, and they coexist as an important part of my life.

When you are feeling great, it can help to remember a little about the other side and appreciate your time away from it. When you're in a tough place, it can help to remember the light of past and future, and that it's as real as anything else. If you are in pain, it's your time to breathe through the experience until you find another feeling. If you are in the best of times, it's time to breathe it in, noticing the hell out of it, because you will need some in reserve pretty soon.

Whether it is a time of celebrating or grieving, thriving or enduring, there is something to gain in our being aware of what lies on the other side (that little dot in the opposite color). We can appreciate knowing there are limits to whatever we are feeling now, knowing at some point the game of tag will continue and the other side will be "it." Being aware that there is a finite time when we're in the worst of our pain makes it bearable. And remembering that our time on the sweet side is temporary can help us savor it a bit more.

Chapter 21

WORK

There is nothing
like returning to a place
that remains unchanged
to find the ways in
which you yourself
have altered.

—Nelson Mandela

*"I can't imagine going back
and telling all of my clients
what happened."*

*"Two of my coworkers are pregnant.
I don't know how I can stand to be
in the same office with them."*

*"I was supposed to be on my
maternity leave right now.
How can I focus on work?"*

Work can represent so many things to us: part of our identity, part of our social world, and how we pay for our home and food. After a miscarriage, stillbirth, or infant death, we may feel like we are in a new world, and the idea of returning to work in this changed landscape can be quite daunting.

Facing our professional lives after such a personal loss can certainly pose a number of practical and emotional challenges. And, as weird as it may sound, returning to work may also have some benefits that help us in our healing.

If you have recently lost a pregnancy or baby, you might be looking at the return-to-work date on your calendar and thinking, *What if I burst into tears at the office? What if my coworkers ask me stupid questions?* or *How am I going to be able to concentrate?*

Every work situation is different, and each one comes with its own issues.

If you work in a big office or interact with a large number of coworkers or clients, even remotely, there may be a very long period when others ask about your pregnancy or baby. This can feel like an endless cycle of being emotionally triggered.

A small, intimate workplace can be difficult in its own way. You may feel that everyone in the office has been so involved in the pregnancy and the excitement of a baby coming that it will be especially difficult to return with no baby at home to talk about. Privacy or boundary issues may also be a concern in a small office. Or maybe a coworker is pregnant or has a new baby, and continually seeing her and hearing about her experience may feel overwhelming.

If your workplace culture is rather competitive, you may feel uncomfortably vulnerable or just "not seen" in your time of grief. A professional woman I know returned to work after her child was stillborn. On her first day back, many of her coworkers expressed quick, sometimes clumsy condolences and then rushed to move on to business. As evening rolled around, a male custodian came in, looked her in the eye, and simply told her how sorry he was that she had lost her baby. She was flooded with sadness and appreciation. That was the first interaction in her workday that had felt caring and human.

The role you play at work can also affect how it feels to go back. If you are in a position of authority, or your work involves public performances, it may feel like you have to be "on" with no room to be emotionally vulnerable. These situations may leave you wondering how you could return to work in your changed and less-than-perfect (but perfectly normal for a grieving person) state.

If you are in a "helping profession"—such as medicine, teaching, or ministry—you may be more comfortable being the one to do the caretaking and quite uncomfortable being the one needing extra care. As a psychologist, I was concerned about taking time off, and also about disclosing my loss when I returned to work. It was not the easiest thing for me to do, and it was new territory for me and my clients. But it was also a relief to see ways that both my needs and my clients' could be present, and sometimes useful, in our work together.

If you are in a role that involves working with pregnant women, babies, or young children, it may be especially difficult to handle returning to that environment. You may be preoccupied with painful comparisons. You may be repeatedly triggered to remember your own loss and to feel acute jealousy toward those whose pregnancy or baby stories are so different from yours.

Just the association of remembering your time being pregnant in the workplace, or knowing that you planned to be on maternity leave at this time, can make it upsetting to return to work. If you expected to be happily pregnant or home with a new baby—and instead you're spending your time at work—this may feel like another injurious reminder of what you are living without.

After such an enormous event, your perspective and values may be shaken up, and work may not seem as meaningful as it once did. It is not at all uncommon to begin feeling ambivalent about your current job or profession. This may be a fleeting feeling, or it may be a crossroads where you decide to move in another direction.

Then there's the possibility that returning to work can be useful to you. Although earning an income is a need and not a choice for most of us, you may underestimate how satisfying it can feel to be making money again. After a perinatal crisis, during which so much has been outside your control, it can be empowering to put in an effort and see the payoff. Doing something familiar with a predictable return can be reassuring. Self-esteem tends to take a big hit after you've lost a pregnancy or baby, and doing something tangible and productive may help you to feel better about yourself.

If your work is generally fulfilling, or a big part of your identity, it can feel rewarding to revisit that part of yourself, even if, like the rest of you, it is a somewhat altered version. Spending at least some of your time at work while you are grieving can also give you a chance to focus on something else. It may, ironically, feel like a break in your day. And some of the routine needed to maintain a work schedule can help you feel connected to the world.

For many of us, work is a supportive and social environment. This was certainly the case for a nurse who returned to her close-knit hospital team after her infant died. Her coworkers made a point of checking in to see what she needed emotionally and to offer extra help if she was having a tough time. They also shared more about their own experiences, and that made her feel closer to them. Although there were still many challenging moments, she felt that she was being supported in a way that made it possible to do her work well and to move through her grief.

All kinds of emotions may come up when you first return to work. The idea of having strong feelings during your workday may be very worrisome to you. But if you give yourself permission to have the feelings and have a plan for taking care of yourself, you will likely find that you can tolerate them. So here's a basic plan.

First, as much as possible, set reasonable goals and expectations for yourself. Don't hold yourself to a high sales quota or schedule a big presentation your first week back.

Many people find it helpful to initially return to work with a shorter schedule or with some days working from home. This can give you a chance to adjust, reorient, and gain confidence.

You may want to make a short, nonworking visit to your workplace before you return officially. This way, you can see and talk with people face-to-face once before you are there in your regular working capacity.

Consider what you would like your coworkers to know regarding the details of your loss and how you are doing. It's likely that nothing will really feel okay, but it might help to think through whether you are more concerned about fending off personal questions or having people not acknowledge your loss at all.

You may want to ask a point person to communicate on your behalf before you return to work. This person can relay the information you would like your coworkers to know about what has happened and what would be helpful to you. Sometimes the trusted coworker can set the tone and let people know whether you want to be asked personal questions about your loss. Your point person may also be able to pass on other suggestions or requests about how your coworkers can help you—both emotionally and practically—as you make your transition back.

Even with this groundwork laid, you'll probably want to be ready for insensitive questions and awkward statements of sympathy. If you don't get them, that's great. But since it's likely that you will, it could be useful to come prepared with a response like "Thank you for understanding that I don't want to talk about that right now."

Once you're back at work, it can help to take mini-breaks or escapes in your workday. Especially in the first few weeks, you may want to plan walks, phone calls to a loved one, or check-ins with a trusted coworker.

If your loss shifted your perspective in a way that has you questioning where you work or what kind of work you do, consider your short-term versus long-term goals. You may not be sure at this moment what you want to do. Unless you have a clear sense of being done with your workplace or line of work, and the household can tolerate the financial disruption, you may want to let the stability of your current work carry you for a while. It's okay to start in one direction and change later if that's the right thing for you.

As always, keep breathing and have some compassion for yourself. You've survived a lot so far. Are there things that have helped you along the way? Keep leaning on those supports. This is an excellent time to practice every self-care technique you know and to ask for help when you need it.

Chapter 22

SELF-CARE

When the well is dry,
we know the worth
of water.

—Benjamin Franklin

"I don't feel like eating."

"Whatever.
It doesn't matter what I do now."

"I have no idea what will make me feel better."

Self-care can be a challenge for us in the best of times. In the midst of the belly-crawling period of acute grief, we may not perceive that we even have a choice when it comes to improving how we feel in this day or this moment, and we may wonder if caring for ourselves even matters. After our loss, we may have a long, hard slog just to get through the hours. Energy may be in short supply, and we may feel that we've lost our ability to focus. A day crying in bed may just have to be our day.

But sooner or later, we will have some choices. We'll have to decide whether to eat yogurt or ice cream, whether to pick up the phone when a friend calls, whether to make an attempt to stretch our bodies aching from lack of movement. We might also notice not just how life has treated us, but how we are treating ourselves.

Deciding to care for yourself can sound daunting. If that's the case, you don't need to frame it this way.

Because just as you only need to live one hour or one breath at a time, you only need to make one little choice at a time.

Noticing choices about caring for yourself is a step toward having a bit of control over your life. That ounce of control may, in itself, serve a purpose for you right now. It can give you confidence. You can start very small and scale up. You can have short-term and long-term goals. You can make mistakes and start again (and again). And you can work in the realms of both the physical and the emotional.

Eating is a basic need that can be disrupted by baby loss. You may be coping with a physical recovery, and your body may feel changed and wounded by the loss in a way that affects how you feel about eating. Your appetite may be increased, decreased, or erratic. You may not have the bandwidth to do much in the way of food preparation.

This is probably not a time to aim for perfect nutrition, but you can help yourself by periodically checking in with your body to notice when you need water and food, and just doing your best. Small bits of protein may help. If drinking a smoothie is easier than eating a meal, do that. Do it because you need to carry yourself through this, and that means focusing on the basics until they become easier. Allow friends and family to help you.

Sleeping can be another strange experience after loss. It may feel like an escape that you want to keep retreating to, or it may be something that is continually interrupted by bad dreams or frequent awakenings. Grief is exhausting, and you may need more sleep. It can be useful to acknowledge this and let yourself have the rest you need when you can. You may not be getting eight hours of perfect sleep each night, so let yourself take naps or sleep in.

Avoiding or minimizing alcohol, recreational marijuana, and other substances can be important, since the negative consequences often outweigh whatever short break you may get. It can be useful to move your body, even starting with small stretches or walking around the house. Taking stock of your physical and mental condition, and considering whether a physical check-up or a mental health visit is needed, is a way of caring for yourself too.

Some of your choices are more subtle in terms of how you treat yourself. One choice can be to consider self-compassion—to practice seeing yourself with respect and attending to your needs with kindness. Attempting to tune in to this line of thinking can help you stitch together one decision and then another. Even small decisions can add up to enough pieces to help you hold together in the world right now.

Opening yourself up to your needs may give you more information that will help you with choices and momentum. For instance, you may get in touch with a need to do something creative, and then find relief as you begin to draw or paint. Or you may find that you are ready to spend time outside or connect with others.

Considering that you are someone of worth who feels pain—and also a person who can notice some space and grace in her pain—may be a useful shift in your thinking. It can broaden your world. A sliver of relief may turn into a slice of feeling calmer and less desperate.

We all have our own dynamic with grief. We have moments when we feel it has power over us. Yet you are still here, and you still have some choices. Taking care of yourself as best you can in this moment is the key to getting to the next moment and to the place where you feel better.

Chapter 23

SUPPORT

Until we can receive
with an open heart,
we're never really
giving with an open
heart. When we attach
judgment to receiving
help, we knowingly or
unknowingly attach
judgment to giving help.

—Brené Brown

*"I sometimes think about calling a friend,
but I'm not sure anyone wants to
spend time with me right now."*

*"My coworkers look nervous when
they ask me how I'm doing."*

*"Our families were really supportive
at the beginning, but now
they don't even mention the baby
and what happened."*

Humans are social creatures. We need each other. We mingle in all kinds of family and work groups. We've developed complex, interdependent systems to take care of each other when it comes to food, health care, entertainment, safety, and emotional well-being. Just to get through a routine day, we usually require quite a bit of assistance from other people. We need them to drive the bus on our morning commutes, sell us coffee, and go for a walk with us at lunchtime to discuss our new favorite TV series. We depend on family, friends, and professionals to help us stay upright and healthy in the world.

During pregnancy, and in anticipation of birth and the early time with a baby, we generally receive even more practical and emotional help from others. This often means more contact with and attention from loved ones as well as doctors, midwives, doulas, and so on. People often meet us with high energy and open hearts during the exciting time of transitioning to becoming parents or extending a family.

When something goes wrong, however, the team of friends, family, and professionals that was very well prepared for a living baby may not be as up to the task of coping with a loss. People may be unsure in their attempts to reach out. They show up at first and then back away pretty quickly, or they may have trouble offering anything at all.

There are probably lots of reasons for this. We don't expect the early end of a pregnancy or the death of a baby, and each person struggles with his or her own reaction. If the circumstances of our loss included disastrous news about our baby's health and the need for a genetic termination, we may be grappling with judgments from others as well as our own complicated feelings about having been put in such an impossible position.

We live in a society that tends to minimize grief in general and baby loss in particular. There is confusion about the significance of losing someone who was not really well known to the world. Those who were eager to help with a new life may not be ready to help with pain and emptiness. This can be challenging on both sides. It can be tough for others to give us support after baby loss, and it may be tough for us to receive it.

Because of anxiety, mistaken assumptions, or just feeling at a loss for words, it can be hard for those who are in a position to help us to do so effectively. And it may feel way beyond our capacity to help them help us. The result can be a challenging cycle. Family and friends might wait for cues from us that they either don't see or misread. The discomfort of members of our potential support system is often relayed through unclear or unhelpful communication. "Let me know if you need anything" can feel like a pretty vague statement to us. If those around us decide that "I should wait for her to bring it up," it may translate to us as indifference.

Our medical providers may also feel challenged in this situation. They are not always comfortable with the shift in focus from more routine pregnancy and baby care to the raw feelings and needs of someone experiencing perinatal bereavement.

Most of us are horrified by the thought of being the neon-lit person of the recent tragedy. It's tough to be that person in the social circle, even as a temporary identity. It's one of the many things you probably wish wasn't happening right now.

Since the emotional and physical ramifications
of baby loss often go undiscussed, you may not
feel socially entitled to being seen and treated as a
bereaved person. You may have trouble letting others
know your feelings or needs. If you experienced an
early miscarriage or termination due to a devastating
medical diagnosis, you may not even want to let others
know that it happened.

Losing a baby means losing someone dear to you,
often in an unexpected and traumatic way. When this
happens to you, it's a high-needs time. Maybe you want
to talk and maybe you don't, but you need *something*.
Maybe it's someone to help you deal with your
insurance paperwork, take you to your appointments,
bring you groceries, or sit with you in silence. Maybe
you don't know what you need, but that doesn't make
you less needy. You're hurting, and it's your time to
lean on others a bit.

If someone is offering help, try to take him or her up
on it. If that seems hard, you can start with something
very small. If someone has to be told that you need him
or her, consider doing so. Sometimes people appreciate
the information and can step up when prompted. Many
people are worried and uncertain about how to be
helpful or whether their help is even welcome. Letting
your support people know what you need may make

them feel more comfortable because you've shown them a way to be useful.

When your medical providers are not able to give you what you need, consider giving them feedback or switching to someone else for your care. At a time when so much is out of your control, remember that you still have choices in this area. Because it can be so hard to process information at this time, and the information you have may be incomplete, you may also want more than one medical professional to help you understand what happened and what it may mean for your future.

If a friend or family member has been insensitive in their help-giving, consider trying to forgive him or her. You may want to take a break from this person, but try to delay making any long-term assumptions about the relationship. Maybe you will want to break ties or change your relationship with someone based on their current behavior, but it may be helpful to wait before assuming estrangement with a friend or family member, since none of you is in the best place right now. Although it can be very hard to forgive emotional injuries, whatever the cause, it may be worth it if forgiveness helps you feel better and more peaceful in the long run.

Ask those who are closest to you and who are the most competent to engage others farther afield in your support network. If no one is local, try using the phone or Internet. If you really can't find someone to help you in the moment, remind yourself that you deserve it anyway and keep looking. As Les Brown said, "Ask for help, not because you're weak, but because you want to remain strong."[8] Asking for and accepting support isn't a Band-Aid; it's a stepping-stone on your path back into the world.

Chapter 24

ACCEPTANCE

Acceptance of one's life has nothing to do with resignation; it does not mean running away from the struggle. On the contrary, it means accepting it as it comes, with all the handicaps of heredity, of suffering, of psychological complexes and injustice.

—Paul Tournier

*"We keep pictures of the twins in
our living room."*

*"I wanted to have a memorial as a way to
show my friends and family what
the baby means to us."*

*"Talking about my baby in group helps me
remember that he was real."*

I visited the New York City 9/11 memorial and
museum a few years ago. It was the first time I've
visited a memorial to events that were clear in my
memory, albeit experienced from across the country.
The pictures I saw there were jarring reminders of
what so many of us saw on TV back in September
2001—the planes crashing, the survivors running
away from burning buildings, the family and friends
frantically searching for news of their loved ones.

One exhibit featured photographs of people who
were standing on the street that day in Manhattan
watching the events as they unfolded at the World
Trade Center. They were in the middle of watching
a world-altering catastrophe, and it showed in big
eyes, crumpled faces, hand-covered mouths. It made
me marvel again at how anyone ever goes from such

a moment of seeing the unthinkable, feeling the unbearable, to having a good life.

There are some lines in life that we cross and from which we can't backtrack. Those people on the street that day in New York can't unsee what they saw on that sunny morning, and I don't know what their lives are like today. I imagine that they range from struggling to doing quite well. I think about how they did it—how they made room for so much. I think about how others I have known have gone through so much and kept living and growing. How did they ever start on that road?

The word that keeps coming to my mind is *acceptance*, in the sense of that simple and challenging task of allowing into your reality the fact that this is actually where you are and this is what is happening.

I've met many people who have faced losses that they thought would take them down permanently. People who were sure that the unimaginable big awful that had invaded their lives was not a thing they could make peace with—and certainly not something they could do something with. That overwhelming pain in front of us can look like a bed of nails. We are certain that only a cushion—a drink, denial, work, distraction, sleep, something, anything—can make it bearable. We feel a need to steer away from the pain, figuring that meeting it head on will bring disaster.

Being emotionally open to the reality that we wish was so different doesn't seem wise at first. Who wants to get an up-close look at all that pain? But it is the one way to face what we feel and discover that we can live with it. If we don't want to play a lifelong game of whack-a-mole, where our suffering keeps popping up in different areas, I believe that the answer is to live our reality and get to know the part of us that feels destroyed. Feeling it and processing it, through time and with support, moves us to feel something more than our hurt and live more of what life has to offer.

In his book *The Gift of Grief*, Matthew Gewirtz makes a case for what he calls "surrendering but not giving in":

> "... the counterintuitive stance of openness, vulnerability, and engagement with our pain is actually the source of genuine healing—the approach that takes us beyond survival and back to living."[9]

Whether it's called acceptance or surrendering, this is something that can be practiced. We're still going to feel overwhelming feelings and need to take breaks from them. Defenses serve a useful purpose at times. But we can start to invite ourselves to be open to acknowledging the places that hurt. We can practice noticing where we are right now, without filling in the space between what we think we can stand and reality.

How might this apply to the experience of losing a baby?

Tangible reminders of the pregnancy or baby can help us take in the experience of loss. Many people naturally turn to these reminders, and some push themselves to do it in small doses. We might visit the grave, if there is one, or look at ultrasound pictures. Looking at photos, clothing, or baby toys puts us in touch with the fact that it all really happened. Whatever the good parts of the pregnancy or time with our baby were, and whatever the terrible ending was, they were real. It's all part of our life and part of us.

Connections with others can support us and ease our acceptance of the loss. This might mean talking with our partner about our memories of being pregnant or time with the baby. Sometimes people find it invaluable to get support from others who have been through similar losses, which can happen online or in person. It can also mean connecting with other loved ones who reinforce both the reality of what we have been through and the fact that we are still upright and alive.

Notice thoughts that are taking you too far away too often. It's normal to start thinking about trying again immediately after a loss. In fact, it's usually extremely compelling. Other thoughts of the future might also have a magnetic pull on you right now. It's often useful to question how much you're shifting attention away from the present. Are you feeling pressured to jump to a different phase of your life or to tune out information about how you've been affected by loss? Is so, you might want to softly invite bits of the current reality back into your awareness to move toward accepting your life as it is. Seeing the reality of your now won't make your future less. Whatever is next will be made better by knowing where you've been.

It's too late to change the lines of your story to date, and that truth can be fiercely painful. But it's not a white flag of surrender or a form of retreat to accept your life in all of its alarming reality. Instead, it's another way to practice compassion and respect for yourself while continuing to heal and grow.

Chapter 25

IMPERMANENCE

Anyone who has
lost something they
thought was theirs
forever finally comes
to realize that nothing
really belongs to them.

—Paulo Coelho

"My life changed in a day."

"Now I know anything can happen."

*"I realize that all I have for sure
is right now."*

A while back there was a lunar eclipse that coincided
with a supermoon. On the Pacific coast, the show
in the sky happened at a reasonable hour, and the
hillside park near my house was packed with people
eager to witness it. Sitting with my partner and our
two agitated dogs (apparently people in the Bay Area
like to howl at full-moon events), I realized that I had
missed a call from my mother.

Later, during a quieter moment, I was able to hear
her voicemail. My mother sounded happy, with a bit of
an excited edge. She said that she, my father, and my
uncle were all in the car and pulled over so that they
could watch the moon above a field. The three of them
live in the same Midwestern town and are in their
seventies and eighties. At a time when my parents and
uncle are usually settled in and watching the late news
on TV, they were instead out admiring the way the
world (and sun and moon) turns.

In her message, my mother cheerfully commented that either this would be their last chance to see a supermoon lunar eclipse or they would be viewing it from the other side—looking down from heaven— when it occurred again in 2033. The darkened ball in the sky in front of me was slowly shifting and growing a bigger Cheshire cat grin. I felt sad about the idea of my family members being gone someday and at the same time happy that they had piled in the car to go celebrate something rare and ephemeral.

It can be unnerving to think that we are all transients who will be moving on. It's hard for me to keep a lasting hold on the idea that none of us knows when we will be finished living, that we don't know whether we are in one of the longer or shorter chapters in the big story, and that we probably will not get much of a say in the matter.

When we have lost a baby, we may feel especially keenly that life is not about fairness and that our time on the planet is of uncertain length. Many of us have lived through traumatic events and traumatic loss. Many of us live with chronic aches of missing our baby. This makes it all the more notable to me that I've met so many people who, either despite these experiences of loss or because of them, are able to dig in and make the most of their slice of impermanence.

Some people draw a clear connecting line between what they have learned about sudden loss and not taking anything for granted. Sometimes I think we tend to be so fractured after loss that the world we end up putting together has a freshness that invites us to notice more details. Whatever the cause, anyone who is able to see and appreciate the little things in his or her life is lucky. Those who can notice grace, appreciate kindness, and find meaning in an activity or conversation are getting regular hits of good feelings.

I don't know any simple, easy secret for how to find peace with the uncertainty of life, but I do believe we are all having a turn at something. We can't do it all the time, and we can't do it perfectly, but we can practice noticing where we are and what is part of our turn. It may be our turn to be old or young or in the middle, our turn to be an expert or novice at something, or our turn to be heartbroken or joyous.

The turns, unfortunately, are not always orderly or fair, and the pain of our turn may be overwhelming. That's when we might feel the most grateful for the fact that it will be changing. We're all somewhere in this moment and will be somewhere else pretty soon. And wherever we are, there is something in front of us that we might want to notice before it's gone.

Chapter 26
MINDFULNESS

The present moment
is the only time
over which we
have dominion.

—Thich Nhat Hanh

*"When I'm having a hard time,
I try to remember how I got
through the delivery, noticing the
short breaks in between the pain."*

*"Sometimes all I can do is breathe,
and I try to remember that's something."*

*"I'm starting to have some moments
of peace, and I cherish them."*

I once spent some time reading aloud to a family member who wasn't feeling well. Our selection was *Unbroken* by Laura Hillenbrand,[10] the true story of an Olympic runner who was in World War II. It's not the kind of book I usually go for, but I ended up deciding to finish it, since I found it to be not just a page-turner but pretty darn inspiring.

The part we were reading (spoiler alert) involves the main character, Louie Zamperini, floating in a life raft after his B-24 bomber has crashed with the loss of eight men aboard. He is one of three crew members who survived together on two life rafts. After being adrift for twenty-seven days, with the men in the throes of both starvation and dehydration, a plane appears overhead. Unfortunately, it's a Japanese aircraft, which starts firing at them. Louie jumps overboard to avoid being shot, and soon the life raft is riddled with bullets.

The ocean is infested with sharks, and as Louie enters the water, he becomes the intended object of the next meal. Weak and struggling, Louie is approached by menacing, open-mouthed sharks, which he fights off using the information he learned in a survival class— basically to widen his eyes, bare his teeth, and bop the sharks on the snout with an open palm.

As the plane makes six passes over them, shooting each time (and dropping a bomb that does not explode), Louie goes back and forth between shark bopping and climbing back onto the raft. When he climbs back aboard the raft for the last time, he finds his two crewmates miraculously unscathed by the shooting. The three of them manage to save one raft and patch the forty-eight bullet holes in it while taking turns pumping out water and clubbing the sharks that are now jumping out of the water to get at them.

The story stirred up a lot of thoughts for me, and it is currently serving as a model of what a *really* bad day can look like. It made me think, too, about how so many dramatic episodes in life seem to be a mixture of lucky and unlucky events. Another take on the story could be that it's a compelling message about not giving up in the middle of a crisis. And it has definitely crossed my mind that I may want to invest in a survival class.

It also made me think about how, in any challenge, no matter how dire or convoluted, we can only face our issues one step at a time. We can only be where we are right then, doing the little piece in front of us. We can only be right where we are.

Louie had a bunch of things on his mind that day in the ocean, and he was all action, but he wasn't really multitasking. When he was smacking sharks, he was smacking sharks. Not dealing with starvation or dehydration, not avoiding bullets, not fixing the boat or trying to float to land. He wasn't even breathing.

Jon Kabat-Zinn writes that "the best way to capture moments is to pay attention. This is how we cultivate mindfulness. Mindfulness means being awake. It means knowing what you are doing."[11] If he is right— if all of those writers, meditators, and therapists preaching mindfulness are on to something—then our moment, our "now," seems a bit more sacred. What we are doing right now is what we need to be doing fully. And all the moments coming will benefit from engagement with the one we're having.

More aspirational than realistic as a way to be all the time? Heck, yeah. And what's wrong with that?

I was pretty anxious during my last pregnancy, which occurred after my two losses. But I remember a point when I really started to appreciate that there were very few things in the pregnancy that were under my control. I could try to eat well, take my vitamins, go to my doctor appointments, and generally try to live a safe and pleasant life. That very short and humble list was the total extent of my control over the experience.

And sometimes, not all of the time, I felt the freedom of that humble list. I could eat and think about eating (way too many bagels for some reason), take my vitamins, and so on, and those actions had meaning and purpose. The rest of the time, I could try to take up my "now," whether that moment was about acknowledging and living with fear (which always passes eventually) or enjoying a bit of peace or hope. Just as in meditation or any type of mindfulness, I didn't stay in this place. My mind would race away, and I would have to circle back, but it helped. It helped a lot.

In times of uncertainty—which, realistically, is always—this is the only moment we have. If we're in a tough spot, breaking it down is likely to help us get through it. If we're in a great spot, it's probably worth taking in. Yes, we're going to sleep through and space out through much of our lives. But it just might help to notice that we can also jump in and roll around in a given moment. Our "right now" experience may feel like a challenge, a gift, or a triviality, but by noticing it we might live it a little more deeply.

Chapter 27
GROWTH

There will come a time when you believe everything is finished.
That will be the beginning.

—Louis L'Amour, *Lonely on the Mountain*

*"I experienced mother love,
and that has added to my life."*

*"Surviving my losses has taught me more
about who I am."*

"Now I see what's important."

Throughout time and across different cultures, the
observation that the challenge of great suffering can
also lead to positive change has often been made.
This is not to minimize in any way the emotional
devastation of the loss of a pregnancy or child or
any other painful and life-changing event. It is only
to say that from such a desolate place people often
undergo, in the words of Lawrence Calhoun and
Richard Tedeschi, "positive change… as a result of the
struggle with a major loss or trauma," or what they call
posttraumatic growth.[12]

This is a touchy subject. It can be very
challenging and uncomfortable to believe that
something good could or should come out of
something so painful. Specifically, it can bring up
concerns that any positive outcome after perinatal
loss is somehow disloyal to the baby. These worries
are understandable and not uncommon. The idea of
posttraumatic growth can also make people wonder:

*Does acknowledging a positive side to a loss imply
that I would choose to go through it?* I don't believe
so. I would definitely choose the version of my life
where my baby had lived over a chance for personal
growth or any other prize behind door number two.

So this is an area where I tread carefully with
bereaved men and women. As a psychologist, I usually
do a lot more following than leading toward this subject.
But I also think there can be a reason to go there. It's
worthwhile, and occasionally life-saving, to know
that others have been in our shoes and that they got
through it. And it can help to know that some of them, in
making their way through the pain, found that their lives
changed in some way for the better. It also addresses the
concern that many of us have after a life-changing event:
How will I get back to normal? The answer may be that
we won't, and that may not be a bad thing.

What kind of positive change do people tend
to experience after a life crisis? In *The Handbook
of Posttraumatic Growth*, Calhoun and Tedeschi
describe their qualitative research on PTG, which
led them to identify five domains of growth: new
personal strength, new possibilities, relating to others,
appreciation of life, and spiritual change.

I have often heard clients express surprise at
what they have been able to live through. Calhoun

and Tedeschi capture the sentiment of many after a trauma: "I am more vulnerable than I thought but much stronger than I imagined."[13] Having survived something they did not expect to face, people may approach the future with less fear.

When it comes to perinatal loss, remembering this sentiment can sometimes be helpful for those of us who decide to try to conceive again. Trying again after loss is typically a very loaded issue. We are balancing tentative hopes and vivid fears. Faced with the prospect of investing again in a process where we are keenly aware that things can go wrong, we may be able to use our newfound strength to address the fears in another pregnancy. We may feel that we could survive something difficult because we already have. For those of us who decide to not try for another baby, the knowledge of our strength may increase our confidence in any future undertaking.

If something unimaginably bad has happened, maybe the field of possibility can be stretched both ways. Unexpected loss is a strong reminder that life can take unplanned and unanticipated turns. Through both luck and effort, things we wanted sometimes happen, as well as good things we had not thought possible.

Many of us find that our view of the world is broadened after a perinatal loss. We may come to see the event as a crossroads. Some of us decide to change professions to something that holds more meaning for us. Some of us become very clear that we wish to become a parent by trying to conceive again, some of us decide to build our family through adoption or other ways, and some of us decide we will not have children but will attach to new meaningful endeavors in our lives.

Relationships with those who are still here can feel more precious when we're missing our baby. We never know what lies ahead, and that uncertainty makes us want to embrace the time we have with those we love. Despite the stress that perinatal loss puts on a couple, there can also be a sense of wanting to hold our partner closer after loss.

Some family and friends may have offered support in a way that deepens and enriches our relationships. Children, whether already in the family or imagined in the future, may be all the more valued. Relationships with others who have experienced baby loss may help us to understand our new world. After a perinatal loss, many of us discover that we feel more empathy for others in general, making all of our relationships feel a bit deeper.

Perinatal loss puts us directly in touch with both birth and death, and it is a reminder of how fragile life can be. It can bring us to greater appreciation of this life and this moment. Feeling the warm sun on our face, sharing time with an elderly relative, or engaging in a favorite hobby may all take on more value when we have been made so aware of the finite and uncertain elements of life.

Losing a baby often challenges our understanding of how the world works. For some, that leads to a new or deeper understanding of spiritual connections. A man who was raised in the Catholic church may find great comfort in returning to the rituals of the church to process and cope with the loss of his baby. A woman may find new meaning and spirituality in nature and in the art she sees in her everyday world. It is not uncommon to experience an expanded sense of being, which may bring up existential questioning and growth related to our place and purpose in the world.

Those who have suffered loss don't always experience posttraumatic growth, and it's not the only way to get through the experience and back to a satisfying life. However, it can be important to know that it exists and that it doesn't have to be big and dramatic to be meaningful.

Yes, some people will start an organization, join the Peace Corps, or make some other striking change in the focus of their lives. But that's not the road for all of us. We may experience our growth in simpler ways, such as feeling closer to our loved ones, being more self-aware and compassionate, or appreciating our world more profoundly. Whatever the path, it's a part of the journey that is ours to keep.

Chapter 28

SLOWING & ABIDING

In the midst of
movement and chaos,
keep stillness
inside of you.

—Deepak Chopra

"I can't stand to feel this way."

"The whole world seems less safe now."

"What should I do next?"

In the first couple of weeks after I lost my baby, I wrote some poems. Prior to that time, I hadn't written poetry since high school and never voluntarily. It was not and is not "my thing."

One of my poems was basically a fantasy about how I could have "fought back" against the events that unfolded after I got the news that something was going wrong with my pregnancy. In my reimagined version, instead of cooperating with the medical monitoring to determine that my baby had no heartbeat, having labor induced, and allowing myself to be escorted through delivery, I overturned the equipment, picked up a rock, and then used it to shatter the scene.

Looking back more than seventeen years later, I can read a lot into that poem. But the visceral memory is of *vulnerability*. I remember lying in the hospital bed feeling emotionally and physically exposed to the elements. It was this state that led to those thoughts about fighting back. I remember sensing that I had no defenses, no power, and no ability to do anything of consequence.

Baby loss puts us in a state of vulnerability. Not the virtuous kind of vulnerability we feel when we take a risk in the service of personal growth. More like the ground-shaking-beneath-your-feet, house-spinning-in-the-tornado, canoe-going-over-the-waterfall version of vulnerability.

When we are in this place, we are beyond protecting ourselves in the usual and customary manner. The walls are down throughout the castle, and the bad thing—the loss, the hurt, the trauma—can find us. We would never choose to be vulnerable like this. It's overwhelming.

As our crisis begins to subside a bit, we feel some kind of relief, however tiny, as we take our first steps back into decreased pain or more control. From the previous place of involuntary vulnerability, we may switch to a counterpose of action. Like someone in a movie who has just escaped being tied up by the bad guys, we are likely to be, either inwardly or outwardly, jumping up and trying to figure out how to return to safety. And safety at that moment seems connected to moving from where we are.

After losing a baby, we may—in certain moments or constantly—have a strong urge to *do* something. We may also have an intense wish to *undo* our loss, however impossible that may be. We might feel a need to take the advanced placement course in grief so we can do it faster and better, and get back to the life we were expecting. We may have an impulse to begin trying again for another baby right away. Or maybe we feel compelled to return to work as soon as possible and bury ourselves in something other than the pain and fear of our grief.

It is perfectly understandable that, at such a time, we may feel a need to take action or seek distractions. Actions and distractions serve a purpose and, to a degree, can be helpful.

It's also possible that the action that we need most at this moment is slower and quieter than we think.

If you've ever taken a yoga class, you probably remember the final pose, called *savasana* or "corpse pose." We are instructed to lie down on our backs with eyes closed, limbs loose, and palms up, and to release any remaining tension in the body.

From a physical point of view, the corpse pose seems to be one of extreme vulnerability. We make ourselves immobile and blind while stretched out on the ground in public among strangers. Our hands are empty and open. And rather than being vigilant about the whole thing, we are asked to relax. It's a seemingly simple exercise that can go deep. Some say it is a time to let the mind and body process what has happened in the session. Some say it is a time to focus on nothing and meditate without the distraction of movement. I've heard more than one teacher call it the hardest pose.

Richard Rosen says that "In corpse pose, we symbolically 'die' to our old ways of thinking and doing." He also advises us to "remember the words of the great sage Abhinavagupta: 'Abandon nothing. Take up nothing. Rest, abide in yourself, just as you are.'"[14]

After my loss, I was not so much into the idea of abiding in myself. Every cell in my being wanted to resist what had happened. Failing that, I wanted to do something to rush through what looked like an awful season of grief in front of me. I've seen this impulse now in so many faces: the look that says "I need to get out of this feeling—*now*."

Following such a drastic injury to our lives, we may feel the need to fight back with all we have. Not taking action may feel weak and heighten our sense of vulnerability. If grief is going to be a long journey, we may feel like we should hurry up and get on with it. But despite the rush to do something or to feel something else, there might be reasons to take a moment to slow down or be still.

After having our heart broken, we aren't ready to be in the fast lane for anything. It's hard to heal when we're always in motion. Grief is an exhausting time when we need fewer responsibilities and more support. We need time to rest and time to consider how to tend to ourselves in our lives without our babies. We also need to practice bearing our feelings, not just avoiding them. As with a broken bone that needs to be still as it heals, what may seem like a time of extended vulnerability may actually be a time of gathering strength.

So whether we see it as a time to practice getting stronger, to meditate, or just to give a respectful nod to the part of us that is gone, we may need to find a way to pause and be with ourselves for a bit. We may even need to lie down and let the ground hold us as we practice just being. We may need to have moments when we see former parts of ourselves die just a little and witness the passing before we consider the next part of life.

Chapter 29

HOLDING & HONORING

But the truth is, the ten
or twenty minutes I was
somebody's mother
were black magic.
There is no adventure
I would trade them for;
there is no place
I would rather have seen.

—Ariel Levy

"I don't want to forget her."

"I can't stop thinking about my baby."

"Remembering and being sad makes me feel connected to him."

Sometimes I'm asked what it's like farther down the road. People want to know what it will be like after years have passed and they become older and are people who did or didn't have more babies and who have had more life happen to them. They wonder what it will be like after they have lived a long time without the baby they lost. Will the memories of their baby or pregnancy fade away? Will they remain as vivid as they are now? What will they feel about it all?

For any given person, I have to say that I don't know for sure. I can't know.

There are things we know about what usually happens: People don't stay in the worst part of their pain long term; at some point, we return to the range of emotions we are more familiar with. Most people don't get post-traumatic stress disorder after losing a baby. For those who have a harder time and need or want more support, help is available, and it can make a significant difference.

And, as usual, life will continue to involve a lot of fluctuations between the zoom and macro-lens view of our personal landscapes, including our losses.

When it comes to baby loss experiences, we tend to be ambivalent about our memories. Losing the memories would mean that nothing remains of the relationship and experience. The disappearance of a memory, as in the movie *Eternal Sunshine of the Spotless Mind*, would mean the disappearance of part of our lives and part of us. And the too-vivid version? We've already lived that experience, and we're probably terrified of being stuck there.

A memory and its accompanying feelings can sometimes attack us with devastating intensity. This tends to happen more often in the early weeks and months, or in response to anniversaries or other specific triggers. However, these strong, surprisingly painful "grief bombs" (as one of my clients called them) may be an ongoing, occasional part of our lives. These sudden attacks can feel upsetting, but they can also be a time of connection to the baby and an important part of our history.

Some of my clients talk about the need to seek out memories—by bringing up the baby in conversation, poring through pictures, or writing down what they recall about the baby or pregnancy.

For some people, the need to honor and share about their baby is passionate, overt, and integral to their daily lives. (Cherie Golant, author of "My Baby Died: I Won't Shut Up," is "out" in this way.)[15]

For others, the honoring and remembering may be more private, although no less sacred. We all have an interior life that is not visible to the world at large. After perinatal loss, the rooms inside us have gone through some involuntary remodeling. This remodeling may be big or small, short or long term, and, sort of like the Winchester Mystery House, it may be ongoing. For some of us, there's a permanent change in the internal landscape.

My own experience has been feeling that something was dug out from inside me as a result of my losses and that the space has undergone many shifts. Early on, it was more like a situation room. Everything inside vibrated with intense feelings while plans were made, scrapped, and made again to deal with the circumstances at hand.

Now I think it's more a room of requirement, à la Hogwarts. It fits the needs I have for it at different times. Sometimes it is a place where I meet others to hear and feel their stories, and sometimes it is a place for me to sit with my own memories. It is a space where I can feel both what has been carved away and what has been added. It is a part of me shaped by a painful and significant part of my history.

What is the appropriate way to tend to such a place? Exquisite and compassionate self-care sounds like one good way. Some things are forever removed from the interior self post-loss, and some things should never be removed. It is a place deserving of respectful care, which means not overlooking it, fearing it, or forcefully messing with it. We look after it by gently looking inward. Sometimes we may nod to the space, make a quick round with a dust rag, or take a minute to notice the current furnishings. Other times, we may pull up a chair and sit a while because something leads us there and it's a fine place to visit.

Either way, a bit of tenderness and awe would not be out of line here. We can show some deference for our self shaped, but not taken down, by grief. We can remember our dreams and our baby, and respect that we loved them and ourselves enough to make room for both.

This may be a place you visit alone or with others. You may find comfort in sharing memories and feelings with certain people who understand your pain and are able to bear witness to it. And there are many different things you can do in this space. Yearly memorials, journaling, or art could all be ways for you to connect to and think about your baby.

Remembering a baby can also happen in very subtle ways. Every spring, I look for the tiny blue flowers that were in bloom when my baby died. When I see them I feel a small, strangely comforting sense of visiting the events of that time. I think about the experience of carrying and losing her, and the mixture of sad and loving feelings I continue to hold.

Memories can pass through and briefly light up something in us. They can remind us of what happened and how our lives have been changed. They might be reminders about connection, impermanence, enduring love, staggering pain, or the capricious nature of the world. They might be about making it through hell and still living.

You will look back as you move forward. Sometimes you'll smell something, feel something, know something because of where you've been. The part of you that loved and lost someone will still matter. Like the feeling of warm concrete against bare feet after the sun has gone down, your senses confirm what you know, that the glow was there.

Chapter 30

A VIEW FROM LATER

Life comes from
physical survival;
but the good life
comes from
what we care about.

—Rollo May

*"I still have a lot of strong feelings,
and one of them is joy."*

*"Nothing has ever hurt me so much,
but I learned how to show up for myself."*

*"I still miss him like crazy, and I'm not sure
how I got here, but I can say that
my life is good."*

I received a postcard from myself once. It was sent from Burning Man as part of someone's art/gift. The idea was to invite people to write postcards to their future selves so that they could capture their thoughts from the experience and ponder them later.

The man who was leading the project said that he would send my card at a random date, which ended up being a little less than four months later. Given that I had initiated this piece of correspondence and had done so in the fairly recent past, there wasn't much about the card that surprised me. The only thing that gave me pause was my closing signature—"Love, D"—which seemed both kind of sweet and wholly unnecessary in a letter to myself.

Receiving the note, though, led me to think about time and how, through effort and circumstance, we change and experience different versions of ourselves. It also reminded me of how different my grief has felt through the years, and how I have heard this evolution described by others.

As you may be acutely aware of at this point, the loss of someone to whom we are attached is not felt all in one brief episode of our life. Although we usually experience the most intense pain early on, the loss will resonate at varying pitch and volume through the years. There is a part of our love and loss that is put in our life for keeps. However, the way we think and feel about it is likely to change quite a bit.

Losing a baby often sets a line of before and after in our personal story. We change to a "new normal," and then we change again. How the loss of our baby hits us emotionally and what it means to the arc of our life may be drastically different one month, one year, or ten-plus years later. Major loss is a crisis that shakes and breaks a certain story of what is supposed to happen. The vision of who we were and where we thought we were going is altered.

When I reflect on my own pregnancies and losses, I can recall very different versions of how I saw the world and my place in it. There was a time when I looked at my future with the expectation that I would be raising a daughter. There was another time when

I thought I might never be happy again. I was so very wrong on both counts.

Clients have told me of similar experiences in their lives. One woman spoke to me about how she viewed the loss of her baby that had happened years before. Initially, she felt that the loss had hurt her in a way that she would never see as anything other than tragic. Years later, the memories of that time were not entirely painful; she noted that they had taken on a gentler, rather sweet quality in a richer life history. In particular, she recalled the internal transition to seeing herself as a mother to her daughter and the joy of the brief time they had together. Although the memories of it were, of course, very sad, they were not *only* sad—she remembered the time with her baby as an important and tender experience.

Both the passing of time and the arising of new circumstances tend to soften some of the pain of loss. You may discover that your values, priorities, or sense of purpose has changed. You may have decided to focus more or less on having a family, or on an unexpected new area of your life. You may have found that you have more understanding of others suffering loss. My guess is that you have learned more about yourself and about pain than you ever cared to, and that some of that information might have turned out to be useful.

This isn't a fancy way of saying that you will just move on from your loss or find closure. You don't have to leave anyone, including your baby, entirely behind, and no doors between you and others need to close. Rather, I'm saying that you will change with time and interact differently with your grief. The loss is not gone or made insignificant, and you don't stay at a fixed point. You will have had a wider set of experiences, including time spent learning to tolerate the loss. As time goes on, you may have more empathy and respect for your former self who went through so much. She may stand alongside you and your current life, marveling at how far you've come together.

CONCLUSION

It is impossible for
you to go on
as you were before,
so you must go on as
you never have.

—Cheryl Strayed

*"Looking back, the day I had my son was
the worst and best day of my life."*

*"My life changed, and I changed, but I feel like
I know myself more."*

*"I have a child who others can't see
and won't know,
but she is still with me."*

I just read Angela Garbes's book, *Like a Mother: A
Feminist Journey Through the Science and Culture of
Pregnancy*. For someone who spends a fair amount of
time listening to women discuss their reproductive
concerns, and as a woman who had four pregnancies
with four pretty dissimilar endings (two living
children with very different deliveries, a first-trimester
miscarriage, and a late-second-trimester delivery of a
stillborn baby), I was surprised to be so surprised by
what I was learning about this stage of life.

It was the last chapter that really got me. Garbes
brings up *microchimerism*, also known as fetal cell
chimerism, whereby cells from a fetus pass through the
placenta and enter the pregnant woman's bloodstream,
becoming part of her tissues and organs—part of
her beating heart. As evidence of this phenomenon,

women who have had sons have been found, after their deaths, to have male DNA in their brains and elsewhere throughout their bodies.[16]

Microchimerism is thought to be commonplace in women who have been pregnant, and the cells may remain in their bodies for decades. Further reading informed me that fetal cells have been detected in women as early as seven weeks into a pregnancy.[17] As Garbes points out, microchimerism doesn't affect only women who have had full-term pregnancies and deliveries; it also happens "in pregnancies that end in miscarriage or are terminated."

Whether or not we are literally carrying around the cells of the baby we lost, the power of that idea as both reality and metaphor is striking to me. The loss of a baby to whom we are attached leaves us in a different state of being. Whether we feel that we lost a person or a dream, the experience has imbued us with something. We may have changed in ways we didn't imagine and don't yet understand. And some of that change may be viewed as growth.

You and your loss stand alone and at the same time connected to all others who have had a miscarriage, stillbirth, or neonatal death. Your individual self and circumstances are unique, but many others in the world feel your pain because it's theirs as well. You own the rights to your own story—what you know and what you're learning—about how you define who or what you lost, what you feel about your loss, the words that fit you and your family now, how you see your identity, and what you take from your experience. And your journey is being paralleled by others around the world facing the same feelings and questions.

So much of what has happened has been out of your control, and no one can change that. The uncertainties of your future remain uncertain. But you do get a very good shot at being a lovely and imperfect person who is practicing ongoing compassion and respect for yourself and your life. Here and now, you are and can only be at one point in your longer-term experience of living after loss.

The road ahead will be hard, maybe anxiety provoking—and it may have unexpected moments that contain sweetness and peace. Your life after loss is still your life, a life that bears scars, precious memories, and the seeds of further growth. By giving some time and awareness to your feelings, thoughts, and needs, you can be the companion you need to the person you're becoming.

ACKNOWLEDGMENTS

First and foremost, I want to express my enormous respect and appreciation for the individuals, couples, and group members who have included me in their baby loss journeys and who continue to teach me about living after loss.

I'm extremely grateful to my editor Jess Beebe of Waxwing Book Studio for her unfailing support and expert guidance in helping me turn my essays into a published book. I also want to recognize Sara Christian for her beautiful work on the interior and cover designs.

A big thanks to Karen Nierlich for warm and knowledgeable help with behind-the-scenes details of getting *At a Loss* out into the world.

My appreciation goes out to my longtime colleagues in the perinatal consultation group for their professional and personal support: Deena Solwren, Laura Goldberger, Sheila Longerbeam, and, most especially, Gina Hassan and Lee Safran for also being a strong and beloved two-thirds of Perinatal Psychotherapy Services. Additionally, a big thanks to Meghan Lewis for her thoughtful and sensitive feedback regarding language and inclusivity, and Ruth Elowitz for her sharp eyes and useful comments on the content of this book.

For her longtime support in life and steadfast encouragement regarding my writing on this topic, I am grateful to Kelly Hulander. For their friendship during this time, thanks to Margaret Mancuso, Nina Senn, Linda Haymes, and Jane Nylund. I also wish to thank Linda Hamilton for being a great friend, an adviser on writing, and an advocate for telling stories about baby loss.

I want to give a shout-out to the East Bay Regional Park District of Alameda and Contra Costa Counties and its supporters for operating and maintaining exceptionally beautiful spaces for me and the rest of the world to walk, bike, and be in. My time spent there was an invaluable part of my process.

An enormous thanks to Sonya Grant Zindel for being my best friend, first reader, and the one who saw it all.

And finally, I wish to express my deep gratitude to Marilyn and Lowell Rothert for giving me a foundation of unwavering love and support; Kiefer and Riley, for all the joy I get out of knowing you and watching your lives unfold; and Richard, for being the best thing I didn't expect.

RESOURCES

Just like everything else in your journey after baby loss, the resources you need won't be one size fits all. The support that works for you may be not be the same as for a friend or family member who has been through something similar, and you will have different needs at different times.

Keep in mind that there may be multiple ways to access support. For example, if there are no therapists who specialize in baby loss in your area, you may obtain short-term phone counseling by volunteers knowledgeable in this type of grief or find a trained mentor who has had a perinatal loss (see "Free Phone and Online Individual Support").

If you do not have the financial resources yourself to pay for a guided retreat with others who have experienced baby loss, you might find help through a scholarship, crowdfunding, donations of frequent-flyer points from someone in your support system, or a loan from a family member. Books (including e-books) may be found or ordered at your local library, and blogs and online support groups are free.

Also, October is Pregnancy and Infant Loss awareness month. There tends to be more activity in the form of memorials, retreats, and conferences at that time. You may want to inquire at your local hospital or search online regarding such events in your area.

FREE PHONE & ONLINE INDIVIDUAL SUPPORT

Star Legacy Foundation, a support line staffed by trained grief counselors who have experience with pregnancy or infant loss, plus brochures and resources. https://starlegacyfoundation.org/resources

Pregnancy Loss Support Program, an organization of trained volunteers who have experience with pregnancy or infant loss. They also offer printed information and resources. A community service of the National Council of Jewish Women New York. https://www.pregnancyloss.org

MISS Foundation, provides HOPE mentors, trained volunteers, family support packets, and more. https://missfoundation.org/support/support-services

HELP FOR THE IMMEDIATE CRISIS

Return to Zero H.O.P.E., provides information regarding needs at the hospital, grief reactions, trauma, and resources for more support. http://rtzhope.org/parents

Navigating the Unknown: An Immediate Guide When Experiencing the Loss of Your Baby, by Amie Lands. Available as an e-book or paperback, it addresses the many specific demands and decisions of a perinatal loss crisis, including telling family members, needs at the hospital, what to do with the baby's things, and general information regarding grief and coping. It includes an extensive appendix with information regarding after-death arrangements, books, and other resources for emotional and physical needs after the loss of a baby.

BLOGS

Stirrup Queens, https://www.stirrup-queens.com/a-whole-lot-of-blogging-brought-to-you-sorted-and-filed Melissa Ford's website of sorted and filed blogs on adoption, loss, and infertility with specific subsections addressing a vast number of topics within these areas.

Still Standing Magazine, https://stillstandingmag.com For all who are grieving child loss and infertility.

Reconceiving Loss, https://reconceivingloss.com
A public forum for personal stories, artwork, and articles on the topic of baby loss, grief, and healing. Option for private support services.

Glow in the Woods, http://www.glowinthewoods.com
For babylost mothers and fathers.

Modern Loss, https://modernloss.com
Candid conversations about grief. Brief essays about a variety of types of loss, with sections specific to child loss, miscarriage, and stillbirth.

SUPPORT GROUPS

Here are online support groups. Check with local hospitals or online regarding in-person groups available in your area.

MISS Foundation
https://missfoundation.org/support/support-services

Share Pregnancy and Infant Loss Support
http://nationalshare.org/online-support

Star Legacy Foundation
https://starlegacyfoundation.org/support-groups

RETREATS

Return to Zero H.O.P.E. http://rtzhope.org/retreat

Faith's Lodge https://faithslodge.org

Golden Willow Retreat https://goldenwillowretreat.com

CONFERENCES

International Perinatal Bereavement Conference, sponsored by Pregnancy Loss and Infant Death Alliance (PLIDA) and held biennially. Attended by professionals and parent advocates.

Stillbirth Summit, sponsored by the Star Legacy Foundation. Attended by professionals and parents.

ORGANIZATIONS

American Sudden Infant Death Syndrome Institute
https://sids.org
Provides education, answers to parents' questions, and support for research.

Disease Info Search https://www.diseaseinfosearch.org
A source for both information on diseases and the related support groups.

Perinatal Hospice and Palliative Care

https://www.perinatalhospice.org

Resources and support when your baby's life is expected to be brief.

Pregnancy After Loss Support (PALS)

https://pregnancyafterlosssupport.com

Resources and support for pregnancy after loss.

Resolve National Infertility Association

https://resolve.org/about-us

Resources and support regarding infertility causes and treatment needs.

Return to Zero H.O.P.E. http://rtzhope.org

Resources, social support, and informed professional care for families who have experienced a pregnancy or infant loss.

BOOKS

Memoirs

An Exact Replica of a Figment of My Imagination, by Elizabeth McCracken

Ghostbelly, by Elizabeth Heineman

Holding Silvan, by Monica Wesolowska

Poor Your Soul, by Mira Ptacin

The Rules Do Not Apply, by Ariel Levy

Vessels: A Love Story, by Daniel Raeburn

Perinatal Loss

A Time to Decide, a Time to Heal, by Molly Minnick and Kathleen Delp

Empty Cradle, Broken Heart: Surviving the Death of Your Baby, by Deborah Davis

Healing Your Grieving Heart After Stillbirth and *Healing Your Grieving Heart After Miscarriage,* by Alan D. Wolfelt

The Prenatal Bombshell: Help and Hope When Continuing or Ending a Precious Pregnancy After an Abnormal Diagnosis, by Stephanie Azri and Sherokee Ilse

Social and Political

Motherhood Lost: A Feminist Account of Pregnancy Loss in America, by Linda Layne

Reproductive Injustice: Racism, Pregnancy, and Premature Birth, by Dána-Ain Davis

Reproductive Losses: Challenges to LGBTQ Family-Making, by Christa Craven

ENDNOTES

[1] Kenneth Doka, *Disenfranchised Grief: A Hidden Sorrow* (Lanham, MD: Lexington Books, 1989).

[2] Joannne Cacciatore, *Bearing the Unbearable: Love, Loss, and the Heartbreaking Path of Grief* (Somerville, MA: Wisdom Publications, 2017), 57.

[3] Elizabeth McCracken, *An Exact Replica of a Figment of My Imagination* (New York: Little, Brown and Company, 2010), 13.

[4] Heather Swain, *Luscious Lemon* (New York: Gallery Books, 2004), 225.

[5] Frederic Luskin, *Forgive for Good: A Proven Prescription for Health and Happiness* (New York: HarperOne, 2001).

[6] Gary Chapman, *The Five Love Languages: How to Express Heartfelt Commitment to Your Mate* (Chicago: Northfield, 1995).

[7] William Masters, Virginia Johnson, and Robert Kolodny, *Heterosexuality* (New York: HarperCollins, 1994).

[8] Les Brown, *Conversations on Success II* (Sevierville, TN: Insight Publishing, 2004), 9.

[9] Matthew Gewirtz, *The Gift of Grief: Finding Peace, Transformation, and Renewed Life after Great Sorrow* (Berkeley, CA: Celestial Arts, 2008), 107.

[10] Laura Hillenbrand, *Unbroken* (New York: Random House, 2014).

[11] Jon Kabat-Zinn, *Wherever You Go, There You Are* (New York: Hyperion, 1994), 17.

[12] Lawrence Calhoun and Richard Tedeschi, "The Positive Lessons of Loss," in *Meaning Reconstruction and the Experience of Loss*, edited by Robert Neimeyer (Washington, DC: American Psychological Association, 2001), 158.

[13] Lawrence Calhoun and Richard Tedeschi, *The Handbook of Posttraumatic Growth: Research and Practice* (New York: Routledge, 2001), 5.

[14] Richard Rosen, "Purpose of Corpse Pose," *Yoga Journal* (August 28, 2007), https://www.yogajournal.com/practice/purpose-of-corpse-pose.

[15] Cherie Golant, "My Baby Died: I Won't Shut Up." *We Are 40* (February 17, 2015), https://medium.com/now-we-are-forty/my-baby-died-and-i-cant-shut-up-about-it-42e2bba4fc79.

[16] Angela Garbes, *Like a Mother: A Feminist Journey Through the Science and Culture of Pregnancy* (New York: HarperCollins, 2018).

[17] Carl Zimmer, "A Pregnancy Souvenir: Cells That Are Not Your Own," *New York Times* (September 10, 2015).

Made in the USA
Las Vegas, NV
03 May 2021